A Special Gift

To

____

From

____

Date

____

Message

____

____

Quiet Moments

Maretha Maartens

CHRISTIAN ART
Vereeniging

QUIET MOMENTS

By Maretha Maartens

English Text © Christian Art
P.O. Box 1599
VEREENIGING
1930

Translated by Sugnèt Kannemeyer.

ISBN No. 1-86852-040-4

JANUARY

JANUARY 1

One Step Closer

"Come near to God and he will come near to you."
JAMES 4:8

Let us begin this year with one of God's promises: "Come near to God and he will come near to you." Take one little step towards him, and his father's arms will reach out to pick you up like an earthly father waiting for his child to run into his arms so that he can hold him against his heart.

JANUARY 2

Gentle Jesus?

"'Then neither do I condemn you ...'"
JOHN 8:10, 11

To our generation, abortions and marital conflicts are very common. We forget about our parents in retirement villages, watching television is our one and only passion and we would rather colour our hair than study God's word. Jesus says - and He is not only merely gentle, but inconceivably merciful: "Go now and leave your life of sin."

JANUARY 3

To Harvest Love

"Sow for yourselves righteousness, reap the fruit of unfailing love ..."
HOSEA 10:12

Suddenly we know: our obsession with money, the breaking of the Sabbath, this life where everything depends on me, these things are not within God's will. Now there is only one alternative: " ... seek the LORD until he comes and showers righteousness on you" *(Hosea 10:12)*.

JANUARY 4

Daffodils in the Desert

"The desert and the parched land will be glad; the wilderness will rejoice and blossom."
ISAIAH 35:1

What is the most unlikely scene that you can imagine? This land without its squatter camps? Daffodils in the desert? God promises the unlikely. In your life too.

JANUARY 5

Idols in the Family Room

"Now Rachel had taken the household gods and put them inside her camel's saddle and was sitting on them ..."
GENESIS 31:34

Sin runs in families. Rebekah's family was involved in fraud, dishonesty and lies. And you? Are you living a prayerless life? Opposed to missionary work? Scandal-mongering? The bigger our deceit, the more desperate our excuses. People without idols needn't lie.

JANUARY 6

Anti-Sex?

" ... at our door is every delicacy, both new and old, that I have stored up for you, my lover."
SONG OF SONGS 7:13

The woman in Song of Songs kept her sweet passion for the man she would marry. Why is it important to wait? There is no stronger bond between spouses than the mutual knowledge that there is only one bowl of fruit to share.

JANUARY 7

Anti-Art?

"And he has filled him with the Spirit of God, ... to make artistic designs for work in gold, silver and bronze."
EXODUS 35:31, 32

Where does art originate? The answer is given in 1 Corinthians 4: "What do you have that you did not receive?" Isn't it amazing how a work of art which honours God, can lead to personal growth, joy and food for thought?

JANUARY 8

Anti-Divorce

"A wife must not separate from her husband. But if she does, she must remain unmarried or else be reconciled to her husband."
1 CORINTHIANS 7:10, 11

To get married is to take one another, for life, says the Bible. Jesus is opposed to divorce. He is also against sorrow and violence and mutilation in marriages. Jesus is the answer to victory: He creates a new relationship out of the worthless tatters you call marriage.

JANUARY 9

Anti-Casino?

"And my God will meet all your needs according to his glorious riches in Christ Jesus."
PHILIPPIANS 4:19

We say we are looking for innocent entertainment. But we are lying! We are after money. Bags and buckets full of money. "God will meet all our needs" writes Paul. And later: "Some people, eager for money, have wandered from the faith and pierced themselves with many grieves."

JANUARY 10

Anti-Fun on the Sabbath?

" ... If you call the Sabbath a delight and the Lord's holy day honourable ... then you will find your joy in the Lord."
ISAIAH 58:13, 14

Dare to eat the Sunday pudding! The Sabbath is not a divine frown; it is an opportunity to rejoice in the Lord. This joy is like the coins hidden in a steamed pudding. Only he who takes a bite, will share in the surprises.

JANUARY 11

Anti-Everything?

"A simple man believes anything, but a prudent man gives thought to his steps."
PROVERBS 14:15

The world claims our religion is against everything. The Bible says: "Those who serve the Lord, find a source of ... " Frustration? Irritation? No, says Jesus. "I have come that they may have life, and have it to the full" *(John 10:10)*. Anti-everything? No: only anti-scars, anti-pain, anti-tears.

JANUARY 12

Fearful Mothers (1)

"Early in the morning he would sacrifice a burnt offering."
JOB 1:5

Although Job's children seemed so content, balanced, sociable and religious, Job was a worried father. This is a parent's burden: you can never shed the holy concern. Job-like prayers are your eternal responsibility.

JANUARY 13

Fearful Mothers (2)

"When you walk, they will guide you; when you sleep, the will watch over you; when you awake, they will speak to you."
PROVERBS 6:22

If you are a single parent or if your spouse believes that a boy can get along on his own, there is still a mighty weapon you can use if your son is involved in unholy activities. "My commands," Solomon tells his son, "will watch over you." Is your son not equally precious than Solomon's?

JANUARY 14

Fearful Women

"'Do not be afraid of those who kill the body ... Rather, be afraid of the One who can destroy both soul and body in hell."
MATTHEW 10:28

Physical safety is a luxury. It is one of God's ways of preparing us for the big test of pain, suffering, hardship and storms. Thank God for physical safety for as long he grants it. Thank him joyfully for the final protection that the world cannot understand.

JANUARY 15

Bitter or Better?

"See to it that no one misses the grace of God and that no bitter root grows up to cause trouble and defile many."

HEBREWS 12:15

Beware of what goes on in your heart, says the Bible, for it determines your whole life. If bitterness persists, nothing ever becomes better. The embittered person destroys her marriage, her joy in life and her spiritual growth. Bitter or better? Which one are you?

JANUARY 16

Praying and Better

"But what can I say? He has spoken to me ... "
ISAIAH 38:15

The way to God is never cleared while we are lying in the intensive care unit. Hezekiah had cleared the way to God long before his illness. Yes, his body was healed, but even more so his spirit. This, he began to understand, is the most important: to be healed spiritually.

JANUARY 17

Compassion: So much of my Time?

"Then, because so many people ... he said to them, 'Come with me by yourselves to a quiet place and get some rest.'"
MARK 6:31

For those with compassion there will often be no time to eat. The attitude and thoughts in your heart will be tested. Serving the community, demands time. You will only be able to survive if you too know a "quiet place".

Compassion

"Even when they cast for themselves an image of a calf ... you did not abandon them in the desert."
NEHEMIAH 9:18, 19

The stuffy charge-office is crammed with perfumed women in fur coats, women in leotards, women full of apologies. "Put your leotards, your diet drinks, your apologies, your self-indulgence and your lies down," demands the constable. "That's it: it looks just like a golden calf."

JANUARY 19

Prayer doesn't help ... Or does it?

"Again, I tell you that if two of you on earth agree about anything you ask for, it will be done for you by my Father in heaven."
MATTHEW 18:19

Jesus doesn't concentrate on rules in prayer. He gives promises to those who pray. Today we read one such a promise. Anything? Anything according to God's will, yes.

JANUARY 20

Promises, Promises ... for the Year 300 B.C.?

" ... you will call and the LORD will answer ... : Here am I."
ISAIAH 58:9

Which words would you like to hear every day of your life? Minutes after a car crash, while you are considering a marriage proposal or on your deathbed? What about: HERE AM I!? But then it must be God who is speaking to you. He wants to say it to you, you know!

Brides Wear White

"Surely God is good to Israel, to those who are pure in heart."
PSALM 73:1

The desire to lead a life as pure as a wedding-dress is expected of God's children. We sometimes have doubts about whether it's worth it. Jesus encourages us: eventually we will receive the wonderful reward for purity: "Blessed are those who are pure in heart, because they will see God."

JANUARY 22

Bread, the Staple Food

"For the bread of God is he who comes down from heaven and gives life to the world."
JOHN 6:33

You need Jesus Christ badly. And so do all others. Therefore this day cannot be an ordinary day. You will have to eat the bread, which is Jesus Christ. You will have to absorb more of him. You will have to tell others where the bread is.

JANUARY 23

Burns, Burning Pains

"But if I say, 'I will not mention him or speak any more in his name,' his word is in my heart like a fire."
JEREMIAH 20:9

God is the God of fire who doesn't allow us to forget him, who puts his fire between you and the abyss. He brands you as his own, as farmers branded their cattle with branding irons in days gone by. Light a fire in your child for the night when he may need it.

JANUARY 24

Why are Believers Murdered?

"They were stoned ... They went about in sheepskins and goatskins, destitute, persecuted and mistreated."
HEBREWS 11:35

Jesus, Paul, David, Stephen, Peter, the martyrs in the lion's den, were all physically tortured. Why are believers murdered? Because they are believers. Maybe we should ask: Why not me? Are you still willing to live for Christ?

JANUARY 25

Joy, the Forgotten Duty

"I have told you this so that my joy may be in you and that your joy may be complete."
JOHN 15:11

Jesus knows about the suffering of his followers, but nevertheless he talks about joy. Happiness is one of the most certain proofs that Christianity works. Happiness is the language of heaven. Lamentation is the language of the earth and hell.

JANUARY 26

Being a Christian on a Wednesday

"Sing to the Lord, all the earth; proclaim his salvation day after day."
1 CHRONICLES 16:23

How would the song in 1 Chronicles 16 go in the idiom of today? Maybe as follows: "Sing to the glory of God, all the people of South Africa; do not stop talking about God's grace. On Monday and ... Wednesday ... and Friday ... and Sunday ... "

JANUARY 27

Christians in Bubble Baths

"The harvest is plentiful but the workers are few."
MATTHEW 9:37

Somewhere, far away from the fragrant bubble bath, Jesus is looking at the helpless people before him with a burning heart. For few of you care! he says. But later he sits on the big white throne and says: "Depart from me ... For I was hungry and you gave me nothing to eat ... "

JANUARY 28

Deeds are Deadly

"What has happened to us is a result of our evil deeds and our great guilt ..."
EZRA 9:13

It is clearly stated in the New Testament: the colour of your skin upsets nobody, least of all God. It is the colour of the HEART that really matters. Deeds are deadly. The colour of the heart determines the colour of the deeds.

JANUARY 29

Roofs will become Platforms

"What I tell you in the dark, speak in the daylight."
MATTHEW 10:27

Somewhere, Jesus says, the roofs will become platforms. Afraid of the roofs, we should be ... as long as we harbour sin which cannot be exposed on the roofs. On the roofs we should be fearless. That is where the gospel belongs.

JANUARY 30

Darkened Eyes

*"But if your eyes are bad,
your whole body will be
full of darkness."*
MATTHEW 6:23

Is there something more desirable than a soul filled with sunshine? Is there something more dreadful than to carry a soul filled with mouldy despair, spider webs, prejudice, feelings of injustice and anger within oneself? A soul filled either with sunshine or impenetrable darkness is not a coincidence. It is your active choice.

JANUARY 31

Depression and Doldrums

"But we have this treasure in jars of clay to show that this all-surpassing power is from God and not from us."
2 CORINTHIANS 4:7

O God, I am a disappointment to you. I have never realised that I am as fragile as a jar of clay. I am thrown on the ground like somebody who falls off a motor cycle, but you never leave your children crawling in the dust forever!

FEBRUARY

FEBRUARY 1

Honour Him!

" 'These people come near to me with their mouth ... but their hearts are far from me.' "
ISAIAH 29:13

And honour him! are the three most important words of your life. They define your way through life. Add a NOT, and you find yourself on a totally different road. If you give him glory, you will hear his words clearly every day. If not, his words are alarmingly solidly sealed.

FEBRUARY 2

Pure Wool, Pure Christians

"May the God ... equip you with everything good for doing his will, and may he work in us what is pleasing to him ..."
HEBREWS 13:20, 21

Real sheep produce pure wool. The good Shepherd wants to make us people of his flock; his sheep who produce pure wool: fire-proof, strong, spotless, warm; and bought at a price. Are you a real sheep of the good Shepherd?

FEBRUARY 3

First Class Carriages

"Do not pervert justice ...
Do not seek revenge or
bear a grudge against
one of your people ... "
LEVITICUS 19:15, 18

God has no favourites, the Bible tells us. Everyone's best work is like a disposable nappy. Nobody deserves a first class journey. Therefore, while not deserving a first class journey, we should not treat fellow human beings like second class citizens. They are not second class.

FEBRUARY 4

One Life

"I eagerly expect and hope that I will be in no way ashamed ... For to me, to live is Christ and to die is gain."
PHILIPPIANS 1:20, 21

A woman won R100 000. "What are you going to do with it?" asked a reporter. "Oh, I will first have to think about it," says the woman. "This happens only once in a life-time ... I will have to invest it wisely." Your life too. It happens only once in a lifetime.

FEBRUARY 5

First, Last

"Yet I hold this against you: You have forsaken your first love."
REVELATION 2:4

Nothing but love pleases the almighty God. You can bake for the church fete, sing in the choir, donate huge amounts to the poor, support Christmas fund-raising projects in the newspapers ... God sees through all this, and demands only one thing - love.

FEBRUARY 6

Esther and I

"I will go to the king, even though it is against the law. And if I perish, I perish."
ESTHER 4:16

The church is the bride of the heavenly King. This wonderful bond was never meant to make us a bunch of self-indulgent women. Esther's king had to hold out a sceptre: *our* King says we can approach the throne of grace freely.

FEBRUARY 7

Giving Meagrely

"Remember this: Whoever sows sparingly will also reap sparingly, and whoever sows generously will also reap generously."
2 CORINTHIANS 9:6

Do you know that it is a sin to live in a selfish and niggardly manner? That God wants to set us free from giving scantily and doing as little as possible? A person who gives meagrely, actually implies that God cannot give abundantly to his children.

FEBRUARY 8

Full of Excuses

"They say, 'The Lord has forsaken the land; the Lord does not see."
EZEKIEL 9:9

Everywhere people are enjoying freedom: God doesn't see us, we are free to do as we like, free to ignore the great commission, free on the Sabbath, free to write and act and have sex as we like to. Then suddenly, we hear God speaking to us in the words of *Ezekiel 9:9, 10,* and we realize: God cannot be mocked.

FEBRUARY 9

One Cubit

"Who of you by worrying can add a single hour to his life?"
LUKE 12:25

We are free to make the most of our lives: God will take complete care of us. Those who worry themselves sick, do not live one second longer than those who watch the crows with a smile. Instead of worrying, we should work for God: then only will the senseless worries disappear.

FEBRUARY 10

Simplicity

"Give me neither poverty nor riches, but give me only my daily bread."
PROVERBS 30:8

Jesus was clothed in simplicity. His sermons were so simple that children could understand them. His working method was simple and effective: pray, obey, do, involve ordinary people. If simplicity is unacceptable, what is your alternative?

FEBRUARY 11

Simplicity and Sobriety

"Our desire is not that others might be relieved while you are hard pressed, but that there might be equality."
2 CORINTHIANS 8:13

Simplicity doesn't mean irresponsibility. You have responsibilities at home too. Christianity grows in the soil of simplicity, sobriety, contentment and generosity. Are you perhaps disturbing the ecology within Christianity?

All, Everybody, Somebody

" ... for all have sinned and fall short of the glory of God."
ROMANS 3:23

Whenever we hear the words: All, Everybody, Somebody in the secular world, they often mean Nobody. When the Bible uses the words: All, Everybody and Somebody they are always referring to ME. They never mean NOBODY.

FEBRUARY 13

Ow! Enough!

"I cry to you, O Lord; I say,
'You are my refuge, my portion
in the land of the living.'"
PSALM 142:5

We all have our caves. You and your body in a cave of chemotherapy, ... you, desperately alone, in your cave of divorce ... That is where we sort out issues with ourselves and with God. We have no alternative but to take shelter, plead, pray and think. Survival means to keep on talking to God ...

FEBRUARY 14

First Class People

"Your became imitators of us and of the Lord; in spite of severe suffering, you welcomed the message with the joy given by the Holy Spirit."
1 THESSALONIANS 1:6

First class people make the best choices: their choice is Jesus Christ. They do their utmost to love one another and to encourage one another in the most difficult circumstances and they accept God's Word joyfully through the Holy Spirit.

FEBRUARY 15

Related to the Chap with the Weak Chin

"Whoever does God's will is my brother and sister and mother."
MARK 3:35

If somebody has chosen to live for Christ, he is your brother. Even if he is more successful than you are, or physically disabled, or unattractive, with a weak chin. Even if he lives in a squatter camp or in the servants' quarters in your backyard.

FEBRUARY 16

Related to the Snob

"Then the disciples ... asked, 'Do you know that the Pharisees were offended when they heard this?'"
MATTHEW 15:12

Jesus says if murder, adultery, backbiting, and such evil things are in your hearts, your are more repulsive in God's eyes than those who hold their mugs with dirty, oily hands. It is not our fine table manners and our pretended refinement that render us pure or impure, but the purity of our hearts.

Related to Jesus

" ... tell them, 'I am returning to my Father and your Father, to my God and your God.'"
JOHN 20:17

We now live in the sphere of God's omnipotence. We are now part of the family of love. We may now say to God our Father: "Jesus, whom you have sent, is my Brother. I am no longer afraid of you, Father, because my Brother has told me everything about you."

FEBRUARY 18

Is my Faith Okay?

"See, he is puffed up; his desires are not upright - but the righteous will live by his faith."
HABAKKUK 2:4

Faith doesn't mean that one never feels desperate. Faith means to see how bad things are, but to listen for God's voice above the howling of the hurricane. Doing God's work obediently, we are able to survive in the very eye of the storm.

Faith: May I Demand to be Healed?

"If only for this life we have hope in Christ, we are to be pitied more than all men."
1 CORINTHIANS 15:19

The most important is not what we demand from God (if the clay ever has the right to demand anything from the great Potter!), but whether I am ready to pack my bags when God says it is time to go home.

Faith: Will my Children Also Believe?

"Consequently, faith comes from hearing the message, and the message is heard through the word of Christ."
ROMANS 10:17

God will answer our prayers for the salvation of our children. But if we have neglected praying for them before, our children already have scars. It is infinitely better to start telling them about Jesus while they are still young.

Pious, but He Doesn't Care

" ... Will your long-winded speeches never end? What ails you that you keep on arguing?"
JOB 16:3

Does it shock you when your spouse questions God's existence? He is only saying in modern language what Job had said long ago. Don't give him a sermon. Your future as believers, your spouse's salvation, doesn't depend on his fluctuating moods.

Faith: A Nightingale Amongst the Crows

" ... suffering produces perseverance; perseverance, character; and character, hope."
ROMANS 5:3, 4

The crows are squawking around us: suffering is bad, why does God allow it? Suffering is good for our spiritual life, says Paul and he sounds like a nightingale amongst the crows. Suffering is never in vain: it is a process of growth for people who refuse to squawk with the crows.

Faith with a Footnote

"For it has been granted to you on behalf of Christ not only to believe on him, but also to suffer for him ..."
PHILIPPIANS 1:29

We believe a light-bearer of Christ walks with a lamp and people will follow us. The footnote: did you know that suffering is possibly awaiting us? Our conversion will be followed by suffering. Suffering brings spiritual growth, and beyond our pain and tears glory awaits us.

Faith Is Not Just Chit-Chat

" ... The only thing that counts, is faith expressing itself through love."
GALATIANS 5:6

The Sunday-school teacher asks: "What is faith?" "Faith is not just chit-chat," says Jimmy. The teacher asks: "Why do you say so?" Jimmy replies: "My father and mother say they believe in God, but they quarrel so much. My brother says if faith is just chit-chat, he doesn't want it."

FEBRUARY 25

Prisoner 119104

"Make the most of every opportunity."
COLOSSIANS 4:5

Viktor Frankl, prisoner 119104 in Auschwitz and Dachau, said: "The ultimate human freedom is the choice of attitude." From his prison-cell, Paul writes: "All your words should be friendly and be in good taste." He used his last freedom in the way Jesus would have wanted.

Lists of Gifts Are Fine, but ...

"'We have here only five loaves of bread and two fish ...' 'Bring them here to me ...'"
MATTHEW 14:17, 18

This is where the miracle always begins: when one comes close to Jesus and makes everything one has available to God. If one doesn't compare one's gifts to those of others, there is no fear or tension or diffidence.

FEBRUARY 27

Prayer + Prayer + Prayer =

"And will not God bring about justice for his chosen ones, who cry out to him day and night?"
LUKE 18:7

How different life could be if we prayed without ceasing. When our lives become characterised by praying and praying and praying, changes begin to occur: first in ourselves, and later in our circumstances touched by God.

FEBRUARY 28

Prayer, the Subject We Lie About

"To a nation that did not call on my name, I said, 'Here am I, here am I.'"

ISAIAH 65:1

In our hearts we are botchers like the people in Isaiah 65: we do not seek the Lord in prayer. We are looking for better circumstances in life and maths teachers for our children, but not for God. The God of heaven says to us: "To a nation that did not call on my name, I said, 'Here am I, here am I.'"

Prayer, the Answer

"He replied, 'This kind can come out only by prayer.'"
MARK 9:29

Fasten your safety-belts: homosexuality can be cured. If it is the one condition which cannot be cured by God, then he isn't almighty. Which things in your life do you deem unchangeable and beyond recovery? What does Jesus have to say about this?

MARCH

MARCH 1

Sanctification, the Ridiculous Ideal

" ... Do you not know that your body is a temple of the Holy Spirit ... "
1 CORINTHIANS 6:19

Living with God can be quite unendurable. God remains so unendurably close - he firmly demands that we should exclusively share our bodies in matrimony with our spouses. He will not yield to our cunning arguments, for he loves us too much.

MARCH 2

Sanctification: Like Enoch

"For before he (Enoch) was taken, he was commended as one who pleased God."
HEBREWS 11:5

In the case of Enoch, we read nothing about fear of death, because for Enoch death was a crossing. Though Enoch had never seen God, he had lived as if he had always heard God's voice. We can walk with God like Enoch. The question is whether we want to.

MARCH 3

Holy Spirit, Who are You?

"And I will ask the Father, and he will give you another Counselor to be with you forever - the Spirit of truth."
JOHN 14:16, 17

The Holy Spirit makes us more gracious, courageous, friendly. He also makes us more unacceptable to the world, for the world endorses other values. Holy Spirit, you are unimaginably, GOD-IN-ME. You are the One who finally estranges me from the world.

MARCH 4

Holy Spirit, what do You Want

"Do not get drunk on wine, which leads to debauchery. Instead, be filled with the Spirit."
EPHESIANS 5:18

When the Holy Spirit was poured out, all the believers became people of fire. I may never put out the fire; I must keep on burning. The outpouring of the Holy Spirit makes me part of the body of Jesus. Through the fulfilment with the Holy Spirit my body belongs to God.

MARCH 5

Holy Spirit, I am Afraid of You

"' ... do not worry ... , for the Holy Spirit will teach you at that time what you should say.'"
LUKE 12:11, 12

We are afraid of a complete surrender to the Holy Spirit; we suspect that it might be somewhat like becoming a prisoner. And yet: only people filled by the Holy Spirit discover their real identity - what would become of your life if you should decide not to be filled by the Holy Spirit?

Holy Spirit: When will You take over? (1)

"If you then ... know how to give good gifts to your children, how much more will your Father in heaven give the Holy Spirit to those who ask him!"
LUKE 11:13

Only when my rebellious self and I call out in unison, and beg the Holy Spirit wholeheartedly to fill every facet of my life and every pore of my body, only then will he come.

MARCH 7

Holy Spirit: When will You take over? (2)

"Let the world of Christ dwell in you richly ... "
COLOSSIANS 3:16

To be filled by the Spirit, means to be filled by the Word. The Word, the breath of the Holy Spirit, fills me and changes me. When the heart is empty of the Word, the Holy Spirit cannot take over. The Spirit shares a heart with the Word of God, with nothing else ...

MARCH 8

Heaven and Hell: Here on Earth?

" ... her (Folly's) guests are in the depths of the graves."
PROVERBS 9:18

The person who dares to live here on earth without the restraints of the Word of God, is already living in the realm of death. There is only one way to happiness: the way of the Word. There are a thousand ways to hell: they all make detours around the Bible with its relentless instructions.

Children of Heaven

"Blessed are the pure in heart,
for they will see God."
MATTHEW 5:8

Children with Down's syndrome - the little children of heaven - are so innocent and pure. We are also supposed to be God's children of heaven, but of our own free will because we are able to understand his commands.

MARCH 10

The Way Becomes Steeper

"If ... men on foot ... have worn you out, how can you compete with horses."

JEREMIAH 12:5

The fact that we have faith doesn't mean that we will continually see God removing all the dangers and incomprehensibilities from our lives. On the contrary, it means expecting imprisonment, like Paul. It is to know that things can get even worse, but to trust God blindly through it all.

Proud, Me?

"But remember the Lord
your God, for it is he
who gives you the ability
to produce wealth ... "
DEUTERONOMY 8:18

God asks: "Do you know why you are prosperous? I have covenanted to take care of you." We should not see our bank balance, but the ancient covenant we do not deserve.

MARCH 12

Hear! Hear!

"... for they hear your words but do not put them into practice."
EZEKIEL 33:32

Do you do the things that singers sing about in songs? Of course not. It is only a song. And this, says God, is exactly what we do with his Word. After the sermon we continue with our old lives. One day, says God, you will see that I shall fulfil every judgement.

MARCH 13

Ashes to Ashes

"He feeds on ashes, a deluded heart misleads him; he cannot save himself, or say, 'Is not this thing in my right hand a lie?'"
ISAIAH 44:20

Those things which can be burnt to ashes by petrol and a match are not worth taking into eternity. They take possession of your soul and you become absorbed by worldly things, says God. Look what is keeping you occupied: ashes!

MARCH 14

Hope for the Best?

"But if we hope for what we not yet have, we wait for it patiently."
ROMANS 8:25

Which word characterises your life as a Christian? For Paul it is the word HOPE. We *know* that everything will change; that those things which we didn't understand, which required blind faith, will be the cause of songs of praise to God, to him who fulfils all his promises.

MARCH 15

Highways are Nice and Hard

"Enter through the narrow gate."
MATTHEW 7:13

Jesus says: You don't go to heaven as a result of pious chanting in church. You *choose* to go to heaven when you consider all the possible gateways, then choose the Jesus-gateway, thank him that he has paid your entrance fee; and do what he wishes you to do.

MARCH 16

Till Death us do Part

*"For this reason a man will ...
be united to his wife, and
they will become one flesh."*
GENESIS 2:24

You never hide your body, your thoughts, your sorrow, your spiritual life from your spouse, for everything becomes one: your dreams, your future, your spiritual growth. Nakedness and sex are the final symbols and proof of this wonderful unity. This joy can and should become yours.

MARCH 17

Savages and Saints?

"Remember how the enemy has mocked you, O Lord ... "
PSALM 74:18

Who are the modern-day savages? Those who despise and defame the Name of the Lord. Who are our real enemies? Those who mock the King and revolt against him. We cannot divide ourselves into two specific groups. We are often as worldly as are the modern-day savages.

MARCH 18

Ideals and Realities

"A man can do nothing better than to eat and drink and find satisfaction in his work. This too, I see, is from the hand of God."
ECCLESIASTES 2:24

The flickering we call life between two eternities is a time of mercy and choice. You can try many ways, but only *one* will bring you joy and a glad heart - God's way.

MARCH 19

Illusions

" ... that they may have the full riches of complete understanding ... "
COLOSSIANS 2:2

Do not make a single decision without Jesus. Pray and study his Word. Obey him blindly. Let him be the root of your tree of life. Build your life on him: your future expectations and your marriage. If we lose this attitude, we are under an illusion: the illusion that our lives will automatically remain in order.

Day of Inspection

*"... When he reached it,
he found nothing but
leaves, because it was
not the season for figs."*
JOEL 2:12, 13

Jesus arrives inopportunely for inspection. He is looking for a fig, only one. Afterwards Jesus goes to the temple. Are God's children gathered in prayer and worship? We see Jesus' divine fury. We shouldn't bluff ourselves. We shouldn't confuse our bustling floundering with worship.

MARCH 21

Item Thirty One

" ... Return to me with all your heart ... ."
JOEL 2:12

God demands his rightful place; he is the King. He can never be Item Thirty One. The items higher than Jesus on your list ... will they be able to carry you into death and eternity? No? The alternative is to acknowledge him again as King and Number One in your life.

MARCH 22

Something Different

"In repentance and rest is your salvation."
ISAIAH 30:15

"Let the Holy of Israel disappear from our presence!" we cry. His holiness is unbearable. You are fighting too hard, says God. You are sinking like drowning men while beating on the water. Come and stand still before me. Listen: I have something better for you.

MARCH 23

Jealousy, the Termite Emotion

"The acts of the sinful nature are ... hatred, discord, jealousy ... ."
GALATIANS 5:19, 20

Jealousy lies curled up like a green snake amidst greed, pride, a critical spirit, self-pity, anger and a sinful, low self-esteem. Jealousy is the termite sin. The person who is jealous is not a builder: he is a termite undermining and breaking down God's work.

Jealousy, the Hurtful Emotion

" ... We lived in malice and envy ... "
TITUS 3:3

Jealousy is like a two-edged sword which only leaves wounds: on yourself, on others. You will never be free of jealousy? Jesus Christ came "to proclaim freedom for the captives and release from darkness for the prisoners ... " (Isaiah 61:1b). Jealous people are always prisoners of the recent or distant past.

Jealousy, the Impermissible Emotion

"'But when this son of yours ... comes home, you kill the fattened calf for him.'"
LUKE 15:30

We listen, while breathing uneasily, to the testimonies of new Christians. We don't like it. They will not persevere, we think jealously. For some or other evil reason we are jealous because God has called people out of the darkness into the light. We are the older brother.

MARCH 26

God Jealous?

*"Do not worship any other god,
for the Lord, whose name is
Jealous, is a jealous God."*
EXODUS 34:14

Religion is not a pastime for the weak and wavering. God has a Name which we seldom use: *Jealous God*. Because he reveals himself to us as holy and divinely jealous, he demands: absolute loyalty, exclusive devotion and undivided faithfulness.

MARCH 27

Yes, Lord (1)

"You cannot serve both God and Money."
MATTHEW 6:24

If you want to be my children, says Jesus, you will have to take a good look at your possessions. When we say YES to Jesus, our attitude towards our possessions changes irrevocably. To be obsessive about earthly goods is *out*. Making money as if you are driven is *out*. Keeping your whole salary for yourself is *out*.

MARCH 28

Yes, Lord (2)

"Be shepherds of God's flock that is under your care."
1 PETER 5:2

We are all God's assistants: each one of us is responsible for a part of the good Shepherd's flock. The good Shepherd will certainly come again and then all the little shepherds will be rewarded. That is what we are living for. To be little shepherds serving the great Shepherd.

Yes, Lovey!

"Train a child in the way he should go, and when he is old he will not turn from it."
PROVERBS 22:6

It is parents' God-given duty to give guidance to their children: in the spiritual domain, the social domain and in sexuality. Do we really do it? Or do we say: "Yes, lovey ... okay, lovey!" in order not to be branded as over-religious?

Yes, Darling, Yes

"I will not ... sacrifice a burnt offering that costs me nothing."
1 CHRONICLES 21:24

Loving God should be like the love David had: a love that costs something in terms of time, money and yourself. This is also a principle in marriage. The "Yes, darling, yes!" after the marriage proposal should develop into a threshing-floor love: we will have to make sacrifices to one another in terms of time, money and ourselves.

MARCH 31

The little Eagle

"A good name is more desirable than great riches; to be esteemed is better than silver or gold."
PROVERBS 22:1

Solomon realises: it is fatal to lose your sense of values. Wealth is an eagle. It has wings and flies away unexpectedly. Once you have chosen between an unpredictable eagle and a sincere attitude of trust, you have begun working on a value system.

APRIL

APRIL 1

The Job-Season

"Then I said to them, 'You see the trouble we are in: Jerusalem lies in ruins ... Come, let us rebuild the wall of Jerusalem ... ' They replied, 'Let us start rebuilding.'"

NEHEMIAH 2:17, 18

God's child refuses to accept the Job-season as final. The Job-season always becomes the season of faith for God's children. For which season are *you* dressed today?

Knowing is More than Taking Note

"These people honour me with their lips, but their hearts are far from me."
MATTHEW 15:8

Religion is not knowledge of the Bible, or of the requirements for church music or the trivial customs in your church. Religion means loving Jesus Christ, obeying and trusting him in a loving relationship. Otherwise you have only taken note of his existence.

Knowledge Doesn't Come Naturally

"It is to be with him and he is to read it all the days of his life ... "
DEUTERONOMY 17:19

In *Deuteronomy 17:19* we find a rule which every person who carries responsibilities, should know and adhere to: "That copy of the laws shall be his constant companion" *(Living Bible)*. Knowledge doesn't come naturally.

Church-goers can Become Worse on Sundays

" ... Go and tell this people: 'Be ever hearing, but never understanding; be ever seeing, but never perceiving.' "
ISAIAH 6:9

When the gospel repeatedly only touches a person on the outside, it is comparable to the friction of a spade against the same palm: eventually a callus is formed and all feeling lost.

APRIL 5

Child + Parents = Future

" ... He commanded our fore-fathers to teach their children, so the next generation would know them ... Then they would put their trust in God ... "
PSALM 78:5-7

The future is either an area of personal hope with the help of God, or darkness without God. Child + Parent = Future. How close have you brought your child to the only way to the future?

Child - God = ???

"You are a swift she-camel running here and there."
JEREMIAH 2:23

We *want money*, God's children demand. We want everything in life, immediately, like a she-camel on heat, craving for the male. It is not necessarily the world and worldly matters that want us, but we who want earthly things. Think again about your child's future. CHILD - GOD = ???

Wheat-Corns Die

" ... Whoever serves me must follow me."
JOHN 12:24, 26

We want to be parasitic plants, extracting every morsel of food from the church, the sermon, the Bible study, seminars and conferences. "Follow me", says Jesus. In amongst the poor? Follow, without the financial support of charity organisations? "Yes," says Jesus. "That is what it means to follow me."

Children of God's Kingdom

"The workers who were hired about the eleventh hour came and each received a denarius."
MATTHEW 20:9

Have you ever looked with displeasure at hardened sinners, those who didn't want to become involved? And when they did ... how friendly were you? Suddenly you see God: He is above all human criticism. He is divine, eternal, inconceivable and gives his mercy without being intimidated.

APRIL 9

The King's Daughters

"When he found one of great value, he went away and sold everything he had and bought it."
MATTHEW 13:46

The King's daughters recognise a genuine pearl when they see one. They snatch it up, trembling with gratitude. Are we moved to tears of gratitude over the Gospel, eternal life and Jesus Christ? Have we already sold or thrown away the costume jewellery?

Stubborn Corinthians

"I speak as to my children - open wide your hearts also."
2 CORINTHIANS 6:12, 13

The Corinthians weren't nice people. Paul observed rejection, stubbornness, resistance and harshness in their behaviour. When one Christian treats another badly, sin is present in either one or both their lives. This causes sorrow. "Open wide your hearts!" says the Word.

APRIL 11

Strength for Today

" ... Those who hope in the Lord will renew their strength."
ISAIAH 40:27, 31

Have you ever whispered: "God doesn't care about me?" God says: " ... but those who hope in the LORD, will renew their strength." Trust = looking up to God continually. What will God give? *New strength.* Not only teaspoonfuls, but abundant new, fresh, unexpected, incredible strength.

Pitchers Crack so Easily

"When the inhabitants ... heard of everything the Philistines had done to Saul, ... they buried their bones under the great tree in Jabesh."
1 CHRONICLES 10:11, 12

The life of someone we know may break into pieces like a pitcher that has been hit by the destructive stone of sin. The people of Jabesh set an example for us. "There but for the grace of God, go I."

APRIL 13

Crumbs

"'Yes, Lord,' she said, 'but even the dogs eat the crumbs that fall from their masters' table.'"
MATTHEW 15:27

Only a morsel of you, Lord, is what the woman is actually saying. Only a crumb of your power is sufficient. How great you are, and I know it! This is how we should believe. And to those who believe in such a manner, God gives much more than to those who are reserved and wary.

Women of the Cross

"If anyone would come after me, he must deny himself and take up his cross and follow me."
MATTHEW 16:24

If you are carrying a cross, you can carry nothing more. You have to walk with it openly. Christianity is never make-believe or just now and then. You become an example of a reborn Christian to everybody who sees you carrying the cross even as convicts were made examples for all to see.

APRIL 15

Do you Know that Candles Disappear?

"He must become greater;
I must become less."
JOHN 3:30

Jesus must become greater, I less, says John the Baptist. Are you also saying that? Listen: How often do you use the word I, how seldom the word JESUS? What people should see is the Light, the Answer, the Messiah, not the candle. No other style is the style of Christianity.

APRIL 16

Look Again!

"His mother said to him, 'My son, let the curse fall on me. Just do what I say; go and get them for me.'"
GENESIS 27:13

Rebekah could have turned back. She could have confessed: "I am giving you the wrong advice." She didn't. Just beyond the turning point waited all the disasters. Do you see a turning point in your life? *Look again.* God gives a swift moment of choice. It is your turning point.

Take a Good Look

"But you do not realize that you are wretched, pitiful, poor, blind and naked ... Here I am! I stand at the door and knock."
REVELATION 3:17, 20

Is George, the tramp, the most miserable of all living beings? Take a good look! says the Bible. You might be looking even worse, because if you do not have a living, growing, intimate relationship with the Lord, you have nothing.

APRIL 18

Choose Life

"Yet to all who received him, to those who believed in his name, he gave the right to become children of God."
JOHN 1:12

Over which aspect of your life do you have the least say? The day of your birth? For each one of us a time is at hand to make a choice: JESUS CHRIST IS MY LIFE or ... ? Have the courage to say: "Welcome, Lord Jesus ... !"

APRIL 19

Live to Choose

"From the roof he saw a woman bathing. The woman was very beautiful."
2 SAMUEL 11:2

Life involves big and small decisions. If only we could understand that our small decisions could rock kingdoms, plunge people into darkness or put them on hilltops! What will your next small decision be? What do you think the consequences will be? Make your choice with God!

APRIL 20

Suffering: I hate it!

"Pharaoh said, 'Lazy, that's what your are - lazy!'"
EXODUS 5:17

Suffering sometimes follows obedience and devotion. Moses did all the right things. And then? An avalanche of miseries hit the innocent people. You know the pattern: Obedience > Suffering > Doubt and confusion > Questioning God's grace > Rebel against God > Break away from God > Commit sin. Guard against this!

APRIL 21

Suffering: Does it Result in Glory Losing its Lustre?

"'I have for you ... plans to give you hope and a future.'"
JEREMIAH 29:11

Have you noticed the resemblance between exile and life after a divorce or excessive drinking? The lustre is gone; everything is grey. But oh, listen to God's words: "For I know the plans I have for you."

Suffering: Does God Expect a Song of Praise?

"... I ... the Son of Man ... at the right hand of God."
ACTS 7:56

Heaven is open for every believer whose earthly body is destroyed. There is a life hereafter. In the hour of Stephen's most bitter suffering, faith becomes reality. Jesus Christ is standing at the right hand of God. He is waiting for him, he is with him.

Suffering: How could a God of Love ... ?

"God disciplines us for our good, that we may share in his holiness."
HEBREWS 12:10

There are abysses on the way to sanctification. It is because we do not always see them that we protest so loudly when the Father's hand pulls us away.

Suffering: What about Psalm 23?

"He makes me lie down in green pastures ... "
PSALM 23:2

The green pastures and quiet waters of peace do not refer to specific geographical places on earth. It is the place against the Father's heart, against his breast, in the shadow of his hand.

APRIL 25

Laugh, Christian, Laugh!

"I will lie down and sleep in peace, for you alone, O LORD, make me dwell in safety."
PSALM 4:8

There is a smile on the face of a Christian who puts his trust in the Lord. The Christian's laugh differs from that of a person of the world. His smile has something to do with a Person, and with trust that will not remain unanswered.

Love: for God so Loved ...

*"I am the good shepherd;
I know my sheep and my
sheep know me ... I lay
down my life for the sheep."*
JOHN 10:14, 15

We can so easily become blasé regarding the Shepherd. The Shepherd is God, King of the universe. The Shepherd left the Kingdom of the Light to save his flock, unasked-for, for the sheep were too stupid to even ask for it.

APRIL 27

Love: I Have so Little ...

"Anyone who does not do what is right is not a child of God."
1 JOHN 3:10

"CHRISTIANITY IS A RELIGION OF THE HEART." When all is said and done, only you and I know whether our love for our brother is genuine. Where there is love, there is the peace of comfortable brotherhood free of any rivalry. The more peace in your heart, the more you love your fellow-men.

Love: "Tell me the Ways ... "

"Then they ask him, 'What must we do to do the works God requires?'"
JOHN 6:28

"The work of God is this: to believe in the One he has sent." To believe is a refusal to doubt that Jesus is the Son of God. Here is the heavenly bread you have just asked for; he is a person, he is standing before you. "I am the bread of life. He who comes to me will never go hungry."

Love: If it never was ... ?

"Because of the increase of wickedness, the love of most will grow cold."
MATTHEW 24:12

Perhaps there was a time when everything went well in our congregation, our marriage. But then we started disregarding God's commands. And the inevitable result was that our love cooled. How can we rise from the ashes again? By returning to the Word.

Love: May I search for it again?

" ... each one should retain the place in life that the Lord assigned to him ... "
1 CORINTHIANS 7:17

God wants to establish his Kingdom at a specific address; we have been ordered to stay. "I don't want to!" we cry unhappily. "It is a place of sorrow." If you do not stay, it will remain an unhappy home. If you stay and serve God joyfully, you will see victory.

MAY

MAY 1

Deaf VIP'S

"'Oh, my lord,' he cried out, 'it (the iron ax-head) was borrowed.'"
2 KINGS 6:5

Elisha was a VIP who like Jesus became involved in finding solutions for the everyday problems of ordinary people. Elisha had both feet on the ground? No, in God's plan. When we become VIP's who turn a deaf ear, we step out of God's plan.

Loving without "If"

"But I tell you: Love
your enemies and pray
for those who persecute
you, that you may be sons
of your Father in heaven."
MATTHEW 5:44, 45

The word IF should not be part of our vocabulary of love: I will love you IF you make me happy. I will love you IF you love me and treat me accordingly. I will love you IF we speak the same language and look somewhat alike.

MAY 3

Lamps on Tall Posts

"You have set our iniquities before you, our secret sins in the light of your presence."
PSALM 90:8

When God's light shines on us, brighter than the light of ten thousand lamps on tall posts, we can pray only one sentence: "Oh, God, be merciful to me, a sinner." We don't want to stumble on in the darkness anymore. We want to walk in wisdom - in the light, in the Light. But God will have to show us how.

MAY 4

Lies of the 20th Century

"Therefore each of you must put off falsehood and speak truthfully to his neighbour, for we are all members of one body."
EPHESIANS 4:25

Lies in a congregation are like gangrene in a body. Lies in marriage are like cancer cells: they can so easily be fatal. Everything we have can be destroyed by lies. The new person is called to live in truth.

MAY 5

Life: A Prayer

"I desire to depart and be with Christ ... but it is more necessary for you that I remain in the body."
PHILIPPIANS 1:23, 24

"Lord, I am still around because my work on earth is not yet done. Let me be an asset today: someone you can entrust with things. Use those parts of my body that are still usable: help me to live as if this is my first day in your service. Amen."

Life: Think Again!

"Whatever exists has already been named, and what man is has been known ... "
ECCLESIASTES 6:10

We toil and moil on earth, but not only for our daily bread. We eat our daily bread in order to proclaim Jesus Christ. Your life has meaning, even if you are in a wheelchair: each one of us gets one life, one chance to talk about and live for our Saviour.

MAY 7

Life: The Definition

"'I am the resurrection and the life.'"
JOHN 11:25

Here follows a definition of life from Jesus Christ's point of view: "I am the resurrection and the life. He who believes in me will live, even though he dies; and whoever lives and believes in me will never die. Do you believe this?" . Talk to God today about this definition.

MAY 8

Members of the Body, Members of theChurch

"As it is, there are many parts, but one body."
1 CORINTHIANS 12:20

If the whole congregation does not attend the Lord's Supper, it becomes a struggling and crippled body. The more members missing, the more pathetic, the more needy and less serviceable the body/congregation becomes. How often are you the amputated part of the body?

Choices

"Finally, brothers, ... if anything is excellent or praiseworthy - think about such things."
PHILIPPIANS 4:8

Christians have to be selective all the days of their lives. Do you remember how well informed and intelligent Jesus was? How he was never involved in impurities? The very reason for his coming was to destroy the work of the devil. This instruction is for the toughest of the tough.

MAY 10

Body and Soul

"But he who unites himself with the Lord, is one with him in spirit."
1 CORINTHIANS 6:17

Our spiritual lives and our bodies are like Siamese twins sharing the same pair of lungs: if our body becomes unholy, our spirit is likewise infected - if our spirit is infected, our body is harmed. Spiritually we become holier if we are united with Christ; this results in the increasing sanctification of our bodies.

MAY 11

Redeemed and Free!

"I am the Lord your God, who brought you out of Egypt ... "
LEVITICUS 26:13

Sin literally puts you in an undignified situation: stuffing unpaid for items in your handbag, crawling around the gambling machines as a Christian, acting violently against your spouse, shouting at your children ... how undignified we are left by sin!

MAY 12

Change me, Lord!

"... be transformed by the renewing of your mind."
ROMANS 12:2

Perhaps you are praying: "Change me, Lord!" Where does change begin? With God. Where does God begin to change us? In our world of thoughts. There, where everything gets out of control and musty, he brings, in answer to our prayers, a freshness, a new vision, the strength to forget ourself and to concentrate on him.

MAY 13

Tired and Disheartened

" ... encourage one another and build each other up ... "
1 THESSALONIANS 5:11

How are you spiritually? Are you still encouraging one another, respecting those who work hard, and those over you who admonish you? Are you still living in peace with each other, warning the idle, encouraging the timid, helping the weak, being patient with everyone? Are you always joyful, giving thanks in all circumstances?

MAY 14

Tomorrow is Another day

" ... you do not even know what will happen tomorrow."
JAMES 4:14

Too many people have said: "I thought there would still have been time - to play with my child; to get involved in God's work, to be saved, to visit her." To say: "Tomorrow is another day," could be very risky. God imprints the word TODAY on our hearts: "Why, you do not even know what will happen tomorrow."

MAY 15

Don'ts for Mums (1)

" ... teach the older women ... not to be slanderers or addicted to much wine."
TITUS 2:3

Do you think that you will be able to present courses on coping with jealousy at the age of seventy-four? Maybe not? You have never mastered it. As women we should pass on specific ways of life, specific attitudes and specific examples to the next generation. What are you contributing towards your child's inheritance?

Dont's for Mums (2)

"'Grant that one of these two sons of mine may sit at your right and the other at your left in your kingdom.'"
MATTHEW 20:21

Do not let your child grow up with the notion that the Lord's children should just *sit* at the feet of Jesus, or that he is the centre of the universe. or the Sunday-school class. Do not bring up your child on the word *sit*, but rather: *work, serve, sacrifice, self-denial*, according to Jesus' example.

Night Thoughts

"I say to God my Rock, 'Why have you forgotten me?'"
PSALM 42:9

Have you ever felt like a little leaf in the Orange River? Torn apart, everything out of control? Until the little helpless creature sees the rock ahead of the flood-waters. I want to say to God: "My rock ... " This is the turning point. The little creature holds on to the Rock and feels secure. The difference is the *rock*.

MAY 18

Rose of Sharon

"I am a rose of Sharon,
a lily of the valleys."
SONG OF SONGS 2:1

The Lord's flowers, the "flower-women", "spread everywhere the fragrance of the knowledge of Christ ... the aroma ... among those who are being saved and those who are perishing" *(2 Corinthians 2:14, 15)*. A man finds it easier to believe the Gospel if his wife is a daffodil, a rose or a lily.

MAY 19

Of course it's Natural

"But the wisdom that comes from heaven is first of all pure; then peace-loving, considerate, submissive ... "
JAMES 3:17

How are things in *your* home? Is it a home where people are destroying each other and their children? Or have you already allowed the Holy Spirit to destroy that which is so naturally destructive?

MAY 20

Take seven other Spirits ...

"When an evil spirit comes out of a man, it goes through arid places seeking rest and does not find it."
MATTHEW 12:43

Do you know that an individual or a congregation can be touched and cleansed by the Word, but if one then neglects to fill one's life with the things of God, this vacuum then becomes a desirable home for the most evil of evil spirits?

Take one or two Others along ...

" ... so that every matter may be established by the testimony of two or three witnesses."
MATTHEW 18:16

Jesus was a brilliant judge of human nature. Why one or two others? In order to prevent both of you from embroidering on half-truths, assumptions, suspicion and bad attitudes. Jesus wants us to encourage sincerity in one another.

Level-Headed, Modest and without Nonsense

"I want men everywhere to lift up holy hands in prayer."
1 TIMOTHY 2:8

"Then what kind of wife would you like?" the minister asks the despondent man. "Level-headed, modest and without nonsense," replies the man. This is what men should also be like when they become the bride of Jesus Christ. How do you shape as the bride of Jesus Christ?

MAY 23

Harvest Day (1)

"The harvest is past,
the summer has ended,
and we are not saved."
JEREMIAH 8:20

We have a meaningless saying: "Everything will be O.K." Jeremiah knew everything would *not* be O.K. His people didn't turn back to God. He cried. Have *you* ever shed one tear over an unsaved soul? How many harvest times have gone by in your life, and how many summers?

MAY 24

Harvest Day (2)

" ... prepare to meet your God, O Israel."
AMOS 4:12

Is there perhaps a minute possibility that some of the disasters which come our way could be a chastening from God in heaven? That everything is perhaps not a mere coincidence ... that God is talking to us before we have to stand before him?

MAY 25

Impossible! ... Impossible?

"With man this is impossible, but with God all things are possible."
MATTHEW 19:26

Jesus is looking directly at you. Who is the unlikely convert? Jesus is looking directly at you. Have you started praying for this "most impossible convert"?

MAY 26

Time to Sacrifice

"The sacrifices of God are a broken spirit."
PSALM 51:17

God requires praise, a broken heart and a broken spirit, ourselves, the living sacrifice. Would you rather bring something else? Be careful, Cain ... when God tells us directly what he expects as sacrifice, he accepts no alternatives.

MAY 27

Time to Offer, Time to be Drained

"'I desire mercy, not sacrifice ... '"
MATTHEW 12:7

"I am drained by people," this world's problem solvers complain. What does Jesus say? " ... the greatest among you should be like the youngest ... I am among you as one who serves." Serving God is not only writing out an occasional cheque. It implies a willingness to be drained by people. For life.

MAY 28

About Turn, U-Turn

"Restore me, and I will return, because you are the Lord, my God."
JEREMIAH 31:18

There is a way home, says God. It has already been graded and laid out. Come from the side roads: come back home, to your Father. It is a U-turn back to the old familiar way made by God. Have you said to God yet: "Help me to make a U-turn, Lord, for I want to turn to you?"

MAY 29

Daddy ... God?

"And by him we cry,
'Abba Father.'"
ROMANS 8:15

An inheritance awaits everyone who has reverently whispered the name "Daddy" before God. How are you standing before God today? As a stubborn adult or a child who whispers: "Dear Daddy ... "?

MAY 30

Daddy ... Father?

"Yet a time is coming and has now come when the true worshippers will worship the Father in spirit and truth."
JOHN 4:23

Prayer is never the obeying of rules. It is unimaginable freedom, unimaginable security and experiencing the unimaginable love of God.

MAY 31

Immortal me

"He thought to himself, 'What shall I do? I have no place to store my crops.'"
LUKE 12:17

The rich fool lived gaily with his great I am. He didn't foresee that the "I am" would live so long; that the "I am" could even live after death and that, while still on earth, he could have ensured an eternal home for himself. You and your "I am": where are you heading for?

JUNE

JUNE 1

Remember, Madam

"Keep yourselves in God's love as you wait for the mercy of our Lord Jesus Christ to bring you to eternal life."
JUDE 1:21

Remain within the bounds. Which bounds? Stay with your believing Bible study friends. Remain amongst the faithful in church on Sundays. Stay within the moral bounds according to God's instructions. Live within the bounds of the Ten Commandments.

JUNE 2

Unwilling Hands

"'Son, go and work today in the vineyard.' 'I will not,' he answered ... "
MATTHEW 21:28, 29

"I don't want to" is an answer which hurts a parent's heart. What, do you think, is the effect of the words: "I don't want to!" on our Father's heart? God doesn't force his will upon anybody. We have a choice. Whatever we choose, we will eventually also receive from God.

Ovens have Thermostats

"Everyone will be salted with fire."
MARK 9:49

Is the great Potter watching over me, his clay jar? Yes ... "For the eyes of the Lord range throughout the earth to strengthen those whose hearts are fully committed to him" *(2 Chron. 16:9)*. God is also watching the clock and the thermostat. Nothing is out of control.

JUNE 4

Survivors

"Save me, O God, for the waters have come up to my neck."
PSALM 69:1

When we experience adversity, we begin to run around like rats. We try to manipulate things right, to fight things right, to pay things right, to doctor things right, to put things straight. Finally we don't survive. Only by praying, do we experience God's wondrous help. He who calls, is already a survivor.

JUNE 5

War!

"So let us put aside the deeds of darkness and put on the armour of light."
ROMANS 13:12

What you *do*, and not what you are holding in your hand, is your weapon against Satan. Simply live as followers of Jesus Christ: your example wins people for his kingdom, your light banishes the darkness, God's bounds are your security.

JUNE 6

Left-Overs

"'How many of my father's hired men have food to spare and here I am starving to death!'"
LUKE 15:17

Memories of excellent food can persuade one to pack one's bags and go home. Do you give your children good food? Loving spiritual lessons rather than interesting television programmes? We either feed our children leftovers or wholesome food.

JUNE 7

Oversaturated Roly-Polies

"You eat the curds ... and slaughter the choice animals, but you do not take care of the flock."
EZEKIEL 34:3

Ezekiel in modern idiom: You don't give those who no longer come to the prayer meeting a second thought, nor the child who doesn't attend the spiritual meetings with his friends anymore. You don't miss them, because you don't care.

JUNE 8

Overfed Ladies

"But let justice roll on like a river, righteousness like a never-failing stream."
AMOS 5:24

If we rest too much, we put on weight. Too much spiritual rest not only makes us overweight, it also puts us in the barrage of God's fury. It is time for spiritual slimming.

JUNE 9

Superabundance!

"For out of the overflow of his heart his mouth speaks."
LUKE 6:45

An overflowing heart is liberating, glorious, terrible, disconcerting! We only have to listen to ourselves to know how far away we are from God at any specific moment.

Get Up!

"Therefore, strengthen you feeble arms and weak knees."
HEBREWS 12:12

The Word says, "Get up!" Become involved again. Become absorbed in God's Word. Start praying again. Do what you can. Work, sing, serve, get on with your life. You'll see: herein lies your protection and your testimony.

JUNE 11

Straightforward

"Direct me in the path of your commands, for there I find delight."
PSALM 119:35

"Turn my eyes away from worthless things ... " prays the psalmist. To him a worthless life is synonymous with living in a way which is not God's way. It is a life where one has thrown away God's guide-posts and landmarks.

JUNE 12

Palm-Branches are Becoming Scarce

"Many people spread their cloaks on the road, while others spread branches they had cut in the fields."
MARK 11:8

People threw branches before Jesus: signs of emotion, but not of conversion. Do you also strip trees of their branches in emotional moments, or do you think seriously about this Man on the donkey: about what he demands and what he doesn't promise?

JUNE 13

One Cannot Remove Pain with a Needle

"The arrows of the Almighty are in me ... God's terrors are marshalled against me."
JOB 6:4

Job didn't need a needle to remove the painful splinter in his life: he needed the tenderness and love of his friends. Before we talk, we should know the facts. When we have no answers, we should keep quiet.

JUNE 14

Plants that Grow

"So give your servant a discerning heart to govern your people and to distinguish between right and wrong."
1 KINGS 3:9

One doesn't want to wilt as a believer. One wants to grow as spouse, as Christian, as mother, as advisor and disciple. Maybe you feel as young and inexperienced as Solomon. What do *you* request from God?

JUNE 15

Plants that Do not Grow

"You have planted much, but have harvested little. You eat, but never have enough. You drink, but never have your fill ... because of my house, which remains a ruin ... "
HAGGAI 1:6, 9

Do you wonder why so many of the plants in your life bear such poor fruit? Maybe there is nothing wrong with the plant, but with your relationship with the Lord.

JUNE 16

Heap of Ruins

"'A ruin! A ruin! I will make it a ruin!'"
EZEKIEL 21:27

In the book Ezekiel we read about bribery and exorbitant profits, fraud and underhand dealing. "They pretend that I am not there," says the Lord. We are guilty of the same atrocities as the Israelites. It is an abomination unto the Lord. He promises Israel ruin, ruin, ruin! What will he give us? Blessings, blessings, blessings?

JUNE 17

Praise Him, Honour Him

"You who fear the Lord, praise him!"
PSALM 22:23

Our calculations in life are the following: Happy incident > Joyful heart > Songs of praise to God. In this psalm we find the logic of bare faith: Critical circumstances > Anxious heart > Take refuge with God > Triumphant song of praise to the Lord. *This* is fellowship with the living God.

Amazing Grace

" ... all have sinned and fall short of the glory of God ... "
ROMANS 3:23

Even though the gospel is being heard from thousands of pulpits on Sundays, there are still people who describe the way to obtain eternal life as follows: "I try to live a decent life, you know?" Do *you* see anything wrong in these words?

JUNE 19

Turning your Back on Sinai

"Moses ... went up and saw the God of Israel. Under his feet was something like a pavement made of sapphire, clear as the sky itself."
EXODUS 24:10

Everyday we turn our backs on Sinai and call other things Lord. We have seen Jesus on the cross. We have seen him ascending to heaven. We hear him talking to us, but we call other things Lord. We all become Aarons so easily.

Rainbows are not for Fairies

"'I have set my rainbow in the clouds, ... '"
GENESIS 9:13

Do we still remember that we are living in the delicate space of mercy between waters and waters? With the rainbow in the clouds God has temporarily given himself a new role: that of the waiting Father. This period will end with the second coming of Christ. With the rainbow under his feet, God is waiting for us to repent.

Get Ready (1)

"All this is from God, who reconciled us to himself through Christ and gave us the ministry of reconciliation."
2 CORINTHIANS 5:18

The message in our hearts, Bibles and souls is not a trivial matter, but the most radical message of all times. It tells us that the thorn-tree of sin will tumble to the ground and disappear, and that a grapevine will grow in its place.

JUNE 22

Get Ready (2)

"But among you there must not be even a hint of sexual immorality, or of any kind of impurity ... because these are improper for God's holy people."
EPHESIANS 5:3

We have to decide for ourselves how clean and healthy the vine of our life should be. Why should the vine be clean and healthy? Because the vine that is sick and worm-infested, ridicules the gospel.

Accounting for my Words

"'You brood of vipers, how can you who are evil say anything good?'"
MATTHEW 12:34

One cannot imagine snakes in a church. Jesus calls people who spit out evil things like venom, the snakes of the church. People who spit venom and vent their spleen on others, do not have a problem with their tongues, but with their *hearts*. For this problem there is only one Healer: Jesus Christ.

JUNE 24

Accounting for Souls

"When I say to a wicked man, 'you will surely die,' and you do not warn him ... I will hold you accountable for his blood."
EZEKIEL 3:18

In the kingdom of Jesus Christ even our personalities become subordinate to the commission: even introverts become guards. The Lord places each one of us as guard in a watch-tower. Looking over the landscape surrounding us, we see people in serious danger. Our task is clear!

JUNE 25

Accounting for People Who Ridicule Me

"Now what you worship as something unknown, I am going to proclaim to you."
ACTS 17:23

Why does Paul keep talking? In *1 Corinthians 9:16* he explains: "Yet when I preach the gospel, I cannot boast, for I am compelled to preach." Paul knew that he would eventually be accountable before God for difficult people, thinking people, resentful people. The same applies to you and me.

JUNE 26

Accounting for what I have Promised

"If you make a vow to the LORD your God, do not be slow to pay it ... "
DEUTERONOMY 23:21

We live and rely on God's promises. What about *our* promises to the Lord? These are broken, not due to forgetfulness, but because God doesn't come first in our lives. If he is the centre of our lives, our promises to him will be of paramount importance to us.

JUNE 27

It cannot be Extinguished by Rivers

"When you pass through the rivers, they will not sweep over you."
ISAIAH 43:2

In the deep stormy waters of tribulations and suffering, God is simply there. He hears your cries for help. He expects no counter-performance. He carries you through, because he, the perfect One, can give perfect love.

JUNE 28

Reeds Bruise So Often

"A bruised reed he will not break, ..."
MATTHEW 12:20

"A bruised reed he will not break." Yet with this message ringing in their ears, people took up canes and sticks to beat him who had promised mercy to bruised reeds. Yes, we too are desperately clutching these canes in our tainted hands, trying to ward off his holiness.

JUNE 29

Call upon Me!

"There is no one like the God of Jeshurun, ... and underneath are the everlasting arms."
DEUTERONOMY 33:26, 27

Do you think that you are carrying the heaviest burden? Read again the story of Moses. What did he say towards the end of his life? His praise of God became more intense the nearer he came to his death. All his life his circumstances were impossible and he survived only with the help of God.

JUNE 30

Rich Ladies

"Some of the Jews ... joined Paul and Silas ... and not a few prominent women."
ACTS 17:4

In God's kingdom there is a place and a task for prominent women. God loves them no better than women in squatter camps. Heed the tender warning: "From everyone who has been given much, much will be demanded; and from the one who has been entrusted with much, much more will be asked" *(Luke 12:48)*.

JULY

Women of Leisure

"A little sleep, a little slumber, a little folding of the hands to rest."
PROVERBS 6:10

Every choice costs something. Folded hands lead to spiritual poverty. My so-called "tranquil life" is my spiritual death. I can confuse "a little time for myself" with "no time for God".

JULY 2

Sow in the Morning

"Sow your seed in the morning ... "
ECCLESIASTES 11:6

The Teacher also looked and saw that things were looking bad. But he says: "Sow your seed in the morning." Sow everything that can germinate: new attitudes, compassion, tenderness, goodness in marriage. No, this is not the time to look helplessly at the grey morning. It is time to sow new seed.

Sow in the Late Afternoon

" ... at evening let not your hands be idle, ... "
ECCLESIASTES 11:6

Late afternoon. These days grey-headed women are referred to as women of winter, autumn or late afternoon. The Bible says to these elderly women: never be cynical, apathetic, idle, resigned, without vision. However unlikely it may sound, there is still time to sow late in the afternoon.

JULY 4

Together!

" ... if two of you on earth agree about anything you asked for, it will be done for you by my Father in heaven."
MATTHEW 18:19

Jesus wants to heal believers of stubborn individualism. He sends his disciples out in twos and likewise he teaches us to go in twos to a brother who has erred. We are to pray and gather in groups in his Name. That is where he will join us, says Jesus.

JULY 5

Stormy Sea and a Wind

" ... he blows on them and they wither, and a whirlwind sweeps them away like chaff."
ISAIAH 40:24

Look up to the heavens, says the Word of God. See how God keeps the planets in their orbits: surely he is able to watch over you, his child? We cry so desperately in the strong stormy winds because we do not look up to the heavens regularly, every night, every day.

Gentle Sister

"Blessed are the meek, for they will inherit the earth."
MATTHEW 5:5

Gentleness is humbleness: acknowledge God in all my achievements. Gentleness is forgetting about myself: losing myself in God. To live in the world of the gentle, is to live in another land on this earth, a land with a new attitude of heart.

Blessed are You ...

" ... we must help the weak, remembering the words the Lord Jesus himself said: 'It is more blessed to give than to receive.'"
ACTS 20:35

Paul experienced a kind of giving that is unknown to us today. He didn't dish out stale soup to beggars. He gave of himself. He writes: "You know that I have not hesitated to preach anything that would be helpful to you ..." *Give?* We haven't started giving yet.

Satan behind Your Ear?

"Then Peter said, 'Ananias, how is it that Satan has so filled your heart ...' "
ACTS 5:3

"There is a little devil behind your ear again," says the young mother. A *little* devil? Satan is the enemy of God, the destroyer of lives - the desperate lion, prowling around to see whom he can devour. Therefore we need the almighty God every day to break his power over our lives.

JULY 9

Satan is not Sitting on Your Shoulder

" ... while everyone was sleeping, his enemy came and sowed weeds among the wheat ... "
MATTHEW 13:25

If there are no workers on the land at night, if they are asleep, the land lies unguarded in the moonlight. The workers have so many excuses for not being involved in the distribution of Bibles, missionary work and preaching of the gospel.

Satan doesn't take to Flight like a Fearful Dog

"Jesus said to him, 'Away from me, Satan! For it is written: 'Worship the Lord your God, and serve him only.'"

MATTHEW 4:10

We cannot see Satan and therefore we talk to him playfully: "Go away, Satan!" But "Go away, Satan" has no effect, for he only yields to the Word of God.

JULY 11

Say it in the Dark

"I remember my affliction and my wondering, ... my soul is downcast within me."
LAMENTATIONS 3:19, 20

There is only one way of breaking away from the circle of always asking: "Why?" Jeremiah chose between self-pity (if he would have kept on indulging in self-pity, rehabilitation would have been impossible) and blind faith (like reaching out for somebody's hand in the dark, when he assures you that he is there). It worked.

JULY 12

Say it to One Another ...

"Then they hurled insults at him and said, 'You are this fellow's disciple!' ... And they threw him out."
JOHN 9:28, 34

Those who sincerely witness for Jesus Christ, soon become a cause of annoyance. Take courage: Jesus will support you as he supported the blind man when he needed it most - immediately after he was banished from the temple. That is his promise to you.

JULY 13

Say it now

" ... Placing his hands on Saul, he said, 'Brother Saul ... '"
ACTS 9:17

Ananias calls Paul "Brother Saul ... " The day before Paul had been his enemy, but now Ananias accepts him as his brother. It is one of the most difficult leaps for a Christian to take. We now have to call our former enemy: "Brother".

Days of Suffering

*"'... Simon son of John,
do you love me?' Peter was
hurt because Jesus asked
him the third time ..."*
JOHN 21:17

Imagine you are standing on the beach. If anybody would come and ask you to deliver proof that you love Jesus as much as Peter had loved him, what would you write in the sand? This day of suffering could be your opportunity to talk the matter over with Jesus.

JULY 15

Certainties

"Jesus says again, 'I tell you the truth ... '"
JOHN 10:7

CERTAINTY 1: No man knows when his hour will come *(Ecclesiastes 9:12)*.

CERTAINTY 2: Your Father knows what you need before you ask him *(Matthew 6:8)*.

What goes wrong if I do not have these certainties or share them with others? Have these certainties made any difference to my life so far?

JULY 16

See Nothing, Believe Everything

" Faith is being sure of what we hope for and certain of what we do not see."
HEBREWS 11:1

Faith is trust and certitude. It is knowing that he, in whom you trust, is trustworthy and true. His blood, on which you place your hope for eternal life, is sufficient. The promises of his supporting presence, on which you hope in advance, will all be fulfilled when trials and tribulations come.

Be Quiet if You Can ...

" ... No one said a word to him, because they saw how great his suffering was."
JOB 2:13

When Job's friends began talking, they became too smart. We don't have all the answers. Sometimes silence, quiet support, simple prayers and a personal wrestling with God are better than all our clever answers to the unanswered questions of others.

JULY 18

Treasures Are so Scarce

"(The Lord) will be ... a rich store of salvation, and wisdom and knowledge ... "
ISAIAH 33:6

Serving the Lord is the most precious treasure, for those who serve him, find themselves in his holy presence. They are safe and happy, they know his will, and they begin to understand that earthly treasures are transitory.

JULY 19

Guilty, Guilty!

"For whoever keeps the whole law and yet stumbles at just one point is guilty ... "
JAMES 2:10

Attitudes give birth to sin. Therefore the one who fails in one respect, is also guilty of breaking all the other Commandments. If we stumble in one respect, it reflects lovelessness and we are inclined to all evil. The verdict? Guilty! Guilty!

JULY 20

Choices (1)

" ... your voice is sweet and your face is lovely."
SONG OF SONGS 2:14

Has your tone of voice changed in conversations with your spouse? Does it betray your feelings of bitterness and unforgivingness? Does your facial expression reflect the suppressed anger, the self-pity which your spouse cannot change for anything in the world, seeing that you are the one who has chosen to infect your life with all those negative emotions?

JULY 21

Choices (2)

"But the fig tree replied, 'Should I give up my fruit so good and sweet ... '"
JUDGES 9:10,11

The trees in the fable look at themselves and decide what is important, precious and meaningful to them. So the fig-tree prefers to keep on making people happy with its sweet fruit, while the vine knows that the wine as end-product of its existence makes its life meaningful. Who are *you* - and what have you chosen?

Choices (3)

"... Ruben went in and slept with his father's concubine Bilhah, ... "
GENESIS 35:22

When Jacob blessed his sons on his death-bed, he pointed out to each of them how their choices in the past had determined their future. "Turbulent as the waters, you will no longer excell ... " Today never ends today. The right choices have a beneficial effect on the rest of your life. Sinful adventures may ruin the rest of your life.

JULY 23

Sin? Why all the Fuss?

"Woe to those who call evil good ... "
ISAIAH 5:20

"Woe to those who drag their sins behind them like a bullock on a rope" *(Living Bible)*. Misery awaits those who oppress the poor, live greedily and selfishly; who put other gods and interests before God, depend on themselves; corrupt the law and lead extravagant lives.

JULY 24

Sin: I want to ...

" ... I coveted them and took them."
JOSHUA 7:21

Sin works as follows: *I want to*. For once *I want to* say what I think. *I want to* ... rest this year, the Church shouldn't interfere with me. *I want to* ... spend this Sunday at home. *I want to* ... go further, after all, we are engaged. But does *God* want you to?

JULY 25

Get Up

"I sign now my defence - let the Almighty answer me ... "
JOB 31:35

Job is at ease with the Lord. He honours him with all his heart, but has the nerve to reproach the Lord. This is fitting, since, " ... you are no longer foreigners and aliens, but fellow-citizens with God's people, and members of God's household" *(Ephesians 2:19)*.

Send me God, But ...

"Do not interpretations belong to God? Tell me your dreams."
GENESIS 40:8

Where you are at present, is the place where God wants you to be. Joseph, Esther, Paul, Philip and John on Patmos all experienced it. God takes you away from a place if he doesn't want you there. Think about Jonah, Zacchaeus and Elijah. If the excuse that it isn't the right *time* or *place* is no longer valid, what other excuses remain? Simply that you don't care.

JULY 27

We Need Each Other

"The brothers ... travelled ... far ... to meet us. At the sight of these men Paul thanked God and was encouraged."
ACTS 28:15

The fact that Paul was so glad when the fellow-believers visited him at the Three Taverns teaches us one thing: even with God at our side, the believers still need one another. The brothers could have left Paul a message: "We pray for you," but it was their warm embraces and their living presence which encouraged him.

JULY 28

Spiritual Maturity

"We have much to say about this, but it is hard to explain because you are slow to learn."
HEBREWS 5:11

"Commitment to Christ moves people out of the comfort zone." Here is a challenge: this week study one unknown part in the Bible (solid food at its best) and share what you discover with someone else. (This is the way to spiritual maturity: when we start sharing, we outgrow our baby shoes and food.)

JULY 29

Comfort me, Dear ... Cheque Book ... Somebody!

"Finally, my brothers, rejoice in the Lord!"
PHILIPPIANS 3:1

Dear X ... You said the other day: "The only things that comfort me lately, are my cheque book and my schedule 7 pain pills." Dear X, you *can* find comfort in the church. We are not better, wiser or more successful than you are. But Jesus is with us.

JULY 30

Comfort me, Lord!

*"Praise be to the God ...
who comforts those in
any trouble ... "*
2 CORINTHIANS 1:3, 4

In the hurricane of loss and grief, the boat of suffering sails on, with the gospel like a light in the dark stormy night. These missionaries are strange, for in spite of pain and grief, their faces are radiant. Why? Because all of them have made the same discovery as Paul.

JULY 31

Home-Coming

"My soul yearns, even faints, for the courts of the Lord, ..."
PSALM 84:2

Going to church on Sundays is not a ritual: it is the soothing of a deep longing, the quenching of an intense thirst, it is a fervent and loving experience. It strengthens one to face the desert. How often do you come home?

AUGUST

AUGUST 1

Time is like Sand in an Hourglass

"Even the stork ... knows her appointed seasons, ... But my people do not know the requirements of the Lord."
JEREMIAH 8:7

Even the birds of heaven obey when God tells them to migrate, to fly or build a nest. They know the laws of God. But God's people do not accept His authority. Time ran out for the people who heard Jeremiah's prophesy. And for us? - time is running out too.

Time Flies ... or doWe?

"I will watch my ways and keep my tongue from sin ... "
PSALM 39:1

We often say: "Time flies!" Actually time remains, but we fly through our numbered years. David writes: "I will watch my ways and keep my tongue from sin." Are you on your knees praising the Lord for his concern for you? Do you also pray that God will likewise give you the gratitude to give him glory as long as you live?

AUGUST 3

Forgiveness

"In his distress he sought the favour of the LORD ... And when he prayed to him, the LORD was moved by his entreaty and listened to his plea ... "
2 CHRONICLES 33:12, 13

Do you believe that God can forgive the Satanist? Do you believe that he can and wants to forgive your sins, in spite of: a licentious youth; an abortion; two divorces? Do you believe the extent of God's forgiveness?

Stumbling and Getting up

"No temptation is irresistible."
(Living Bible)
1 CORINTHIANS 10:13

Why do you persist in sinning? Why succumb to the anger you are nursing in your heart throughout the day resulting in a quarrel with your spouse when he comes home? You deceive yourself with the notion that temptations cannot be resisted. Pay heed to the text for today.

AUGUST 5

Greatness, Today

"'The greatest among you will be your servant."
MATTHEW 23:11

Could it be that your less talented child is God's pride and joy? This child who dutifully dusts the furniture ... who prays at night in a childlike way for others more gifted than herself? Christ turns all worldly standards upside down. Those who are prepared to serve, are the greatest in the kingdom of God.

AUGUST 6

Views on Eternity

"Whoever believes in him is not condemned, but whoever does not believe stands condemned already because he has not believed in the name of God's one and only Son."
JOHN 3:18

More than one book is mentioned in *Revelation 20:12*. One is *the Book of Life*. This is the only book which concerns believers, because it contains their names.

AUGUST 7

Being a Woman = Being Responsible

"A woman must not wear men's clothing, nor a man ... women's clothing, for the LORD ... detests ... this."
DEUTERONOMY 22:5

The restriction on wearing men's clothes has to do with the differences between the sexes and with the reversal of roles instituted by God himself. Are you reversing the roles? Are you dominating your husband?

AUGUST 8

Crushed People

"But the wicked are like the tossing sea, which cannot rest ... "
ISAIAH 57:20

I know your restlessness, says God. Those who try to cope without God, are like the stormy ocean, continually washing up flotsam. This restlessness, mud and sludge is no life, says God. He wants to calm our sea and stop us from destroying ourselves.

AUGUST 9

Figs in Baskets

"One basket had very good figs, like those that ripen early; the other basket had very poor figs, so bad they could not be eaten."
JEREMIAH 24:2

The further we distance ourselves from God, the poorer are the figs, the less attractive our religion will be to others. The Lord's children are like a basket full of beautiful figs; a feast for the eyes. Which basket is your choice?

AUGUST 10

Forget-Me-Not

"Such is the destiny of all who forget God; so perishes the hope of the godless."
JOB 8:13

Everything may appear to be just fine in your life at present: in your career, business or congregation. But: Forget me not, says God. It can be the most fatal, expensive and tragic mistake of your life.

AUGUST 11

Don't Stop Them

"(The Jews) ... are hostile ...
in their effort to keep us from
speaking to the Gentiles so
that they may be saved."
1 THESSALONIANS 2:15, 16

Are you a trellis gate or a road block in the way of the Gospel? Such people have many excuses for being disobedient themselves and manipulate the congregation to a standstill: "If money is donated to missionary work once more, I shall withdraw my thanks-offering."

AUGUST 12

Preach this Gospel

" ... but he who stands firm to the end will be saved."
MATTHEW 24:13

No believer need fear the second coming of Christ. It is the day of our deliverance: there is no condemnation for those who are in Christ Jesus. But although we need not fear, we dare not become neutral as far as the Second Coming is concerned. Neutrality is proof that our love for Jesus is not strong enough.

AUGUST 13

Unconfessed Sins

" ... even in his illness he did not seek help from the Lord, but only from the physicians."
2 CHRONICLES 16:12

Asa refused to confess his sins. When sin takes root in your life it is not like a boarder whose coming and going is not really a nuisance. Unconfessed sin is like a live-in monster, a dictator, a terrifying, dominating, destructive personality. Are *you* nursing a monster?

Times of Longing

" ... the earth will be full of the knowledge of the Lord as the waters cover the sea."
ISAIAH 11:9

The most dreadful thing that can happen in your spiritual life, is that you can experience a time of drought *without* longing for God. Wake up! Knowledge of God is available to us in many forms: spiritual books, messages on radio and television ... The drought is over. Implore God to make this a time of longing in your life!

AUGUST 15

Deceived!

"The great dragon was hurled down ... He was hurled to the earth, and his angels with him."
REVELATION 12:9

The most shocking and amazing fact regarding man, is that he loves Satan, the lacerating monster, and allows him into his life. The deceiver of the whole world is powerful, alive and active. So often the deceived willingly succumb to his deception. Oh, pray that God will forbid this!

AUGUST 16

Satisfied = Lost (Sometimes)

" ... give me neither poverty nor riches, but give me only my daily bread."
PROVERBS 30:8, 9

Agur fears circumstances which can tempt him to deny God, and pleads for the best conditions for spiritual growth. This is unnecessary. Never again do we have to ask God for that, because: "I can do everything through him who gives me strength" *(Phil. 4:13).*

AUGUST 17

Representative with a Chain of Office

"What you are doing is not good. You and these people who come to you will only wear yourselves out. The work is too heavy for you."
EXODUS 18:17, 18

Leadership and motherhood involve risks. Somewhere each of us receives a visit from Jethro. Those who reject his advice, become self-pitying, burnt-out caricatures of Christianity.

AUGUST 18

Do You Trust God?

"What have you done to us by bringing us out of Egypt?"
EXODUS 14:11

Fear sometimes brings out the ugliest characteristics in a person. We forget about the great deeds of the Lord in the past. We start punching the punching-bag which is closest to us. We lose sight of the ultimate objective. How blessed were the Israelites to have Moses with them ... he trusted God blindly. Are *you* a believer who looks up to heaven in the storm?

AUGUST 19

Confused, Estranged, Frightened

"A new command I give you: Love one another."
JOHN 13:34

Do you know the cause of degeneration, disillusionment, disappointments and conflict in new (and old) marriages? It has its roots in primitive, Old Testament pre-Christ actions. One who gets to know Jesus, has a new example: that of Jesus himself.

Filled Up!

"These things happened to Judah ... For he (Manasseh) had filled Jerusalem with innocent blood ... "
2 KINGS 24:3,4

The man who is not filled with the Holy Spirit, fills his house with tantrums, alcohol and his terrifying personality. The woman who is not filled with the Holy Spirit, fills the house with discontent, criticism, suspicion, moodiness. Like Manasseh, we fill our environment with that with which we are filled.

AUGUST 21

Followers of Jesus Christ

"I am the light of the world."
JOHN 8:12

"So if you follow me, you won't be stumbling through the darkness, for living light will flood your path" *(Living Bible)*. What more do we need? With what would you equip a traveller for life? Jesus gives us exactly what we need: light. Not a lantern: himself as Light for every decision, every fear, every choice, every turn in the road.

AUGUST 22

Perseverance: The Unpopular Demand

" ... If only I may finish the race and complete the task the Lord Jesus has given me."
ACTS 20:24

Paul knows why he is here on earth: to preach the gospel. Perseverance is the most unpopular of all God's demands, because it runs counter to our selfishness. We too know what we ought to do on earth. Will it occupy us until Jesus comes?

AUGUST 23

You may ask

"'And I will do whatever you ask in my name, so that the Son may bring glory to the Father.'"
JOHN 14:13

You need only ask, says Jesus. If you struggle with anything which must be done to glorify the Father, then ask, and I'll help you, he promises. The believer who lives close to Jesus, will have no strange, selfish requests. He will ask much and always receive.

Peace: The Scarce Fruit

"Jews and Gentiles alike are all under sin. ... the way of peace they do not know."
ROMANS 3:9, 17

Where the tyrant named *sin* is in control, one can recognise the voice of the master in the voices of his servants, and see his hand in his followers. The way of peace can only be opened and paved by the Prince of Peace. Only with him can we tread this path. On which way are *you*?

AUGUST 25

Queer Strangers

"... live your lives as strangers here in reverent fear."
1 PETER 1:17

We Christians are a queer lot. And often, exactly because we honour God, we will feel like strangers: a bit out of place, the object of less flattering discussion, objects of observation, the unwelcome. But we know: there is no choice between such friends and our Saviour.

AUGUST 26

Daily Joy

"You will fill me with joy in your presence ..."
PSALM 16:11

Nowadays we count our worries. David counts his blessings: he knows that he can take refuge in God, that he belongs to him. The living God is his God. The better David knows God, the more he experiences abundant joy. Cross out from your list every blessing that God can take away. Aren't there any? Go on your knees and thank God for what he gives you.

AUGUST 27

Fire Keeps You Awake

"For jealousy arouses a husbands fury, and he will show no mercy when he takes revenge."
PROVERBS 6:34

One fire causes another. The foolishness of an illegitimate relationship is sometimes the result of a fiery tongue. When a woman scorches communication with her holier-than-thou attitude, a second fire can begin: the fire of the illegitimate relationship between her husband and another woman.

AUGUST 28

Risk It!

" ... most of the brothers have been encouraged to speak the word of God more courageously and fearlessly."
PHILIPPIANS 1:14

If certain risks aren't taken in your spiritual life, it can cause great damage, spiritual deprivation and sorrow. Dare to preach the gospel, to bring the whole tithe into the storehouse, to love your enemy and to do God's will. Try it!

AUGUST 29

Despair Is Out!

"Immediately Jesus reached out his hand and caught him. 'You of little faith,' he said, 'why did you doubt?'"
MATTHEW 14:31

When is Jesus part of our life? Is he with us? Jesus himself supplies the answer: "Whoever has my commands and obeys them, he is the one who loves me. He who loves me will be loved by my Father ... and we will come to him and make our home with him" *(John 14:21, 23).*

AUGUST 30

Watch Out

"Then, after desire has conceived, it gives birth to sin; and sin ... gives birth to death."
JAMES 1:14

From the impregnated heart, deeds are born. Sin never remains small and innocent. It is like a baby: it grows bigger and bigger. It results in death. Are *you* actively keeping watch?

Truth is Truth

" ... our offences are many in your sight ... "
ISAIAH 59:12, 13

A pitch dark scene is often the result of pitch dark hearts which belong to the prince of darkness. There is only one way in which truth can come to dwell in the hearts of man and society. The heart should become the dwelling place of the Holy Spirit.

SEPTEMBER

Victorious Women

"By faith the prostitute Rahab ... was not killed with those who were disobedient."
HEBREWS 11:31

Victorious women forget the past and reach out for the future. They focus on eternal life. Scarlet woman, mother, martyr, woman in a hopeless situation: with your eyes on God you will be victorious!

Weapons are Becoming Essential

"... with weapons of right-eousness in the right hand and in the left ... "
2 CORINTHIANS 6:7

Nobody can resist the warmth of genuine love nor the tenderness of the Holy Spirit, the unselfishness of a true Christian, the life of faith and hope that you observe daily in your colleague behind the other desk in the office. Bastions crumble before these weapons.

SEPTEMBER 3

Quiet Waters

" ... ask for the ancient paths,
ask where the good way is,
and walk in it, and you will
find rest for your souls."
JEREMIAH 6:16

We say: "Everything is okay," while our homes, congregations and lives are wounded. Something is amiss, therefore the wound is so deep and infected. " ... ask for the ancient paths" (when you still walked with God). The quiet waters are reached via ancient paths.

SEPTEMBER 4

God's Special People

"Do not take advantage of a widow or an orphan."
EXODUS 22:22

Widows, take courage: God cares! And let those of us who still experience the warmth of togetherness, be obedient in regard to our care of lonely people in our community, because God says: "Do not take advantage of a widow or an orphan. If you do and they cry out to me, I will certainly hear their cry."

Pasture for Many Sheep

"'Is it not enough for you to drink clear water? Must you also muddy the rest with your feet?'"
EZEKIEL 24:18

Do you make the water muddy for others? We drink the pure water of a pure doctrine, but contaminate the water by arguments and quarrels, fights, discontent and lovelessness. People look at our lives and reject our religion.

Work is no Punishment

"Always give yourselves fully to the work of the Lord ... "
1 CORINTHIANS 15:58

Working for Christ on earth is never a punishment. It is like sowing new seed which is unknown to us. How big will our surprise be when we see the flowers and fruit in the New Jerusalem!

Cast Everything on Me

"Cast your cares on the Lord and he will sustain you ... "
PSALM 55:22

EDNA, FLORENCE AND MARIA are the names of the modern-day cyclones and typhoons. *Our* cyclones and typhoons have different names: cancer, the pregnancy of my child who is still at school, divorce, bankruptcy, etc. Don't bear your burdens alone. Entrust them to the Lord; "he will never let the righteous fall."

Is it God's Will?

"... be clear minded and self controlled so that you can pray."
1 PETER 4:7

Christians often find themselves in situations where they should know the will of God. If you pray with a clear mind, the Holy Spirit will enable you to know God's will in your specific situation. In fact, the Holy Spirit himself will intercede for us in accordance with God's will. *(Romans 8:27)*

Wounds and Scars

" ... for I bear on my body the marks of Jesus."
GALATIANS 6:17

Have the world and people of the world written you off as a hopeless case? (You can stand on your head, she won't take part in Sunday sports ... write anything that doesn't honour God, act in naked scenes ...) Do you bear on your body the marks of Jesus?

Wisdom

"But we preach Christ crucified: a stumbling block to Jews and foolishness to Gentiles."
1 CORINTHIANS 1:23

Often the childlike, cleansed, strange people as well as tax collectors and prostitutes enter heaven, for they have believed what the world ridiculed as sectarian nonsense.

Jesus said ... 1

"Everyone who hears these words of mine and puts them into practice is like a wise man who built his house on the rock."
MATTHEW 7:24

Ironstone-foundation people or sea-sand builders, these are the two kinds of people on earth. Who are you? The builder in the mountain, or the child playing with a red plastic spade in the sand? Who you are determines what is to become of your house.

SEPTEMBER 12

Jesus said ... 2

"I desire mercy, not sacrifice."
MATTHEW 9:13

You can keep your Sunday collection, says Jesus. Use it for charcoal or pantihose. The show-cakes on the fete table mean nothing. Pack away the books of your church-choir. The music isn't worth the paper on which it is printed. I desire mercy, not sacrifice.

SEPTEMBER 13

Jesus said ... 3

"Neither do men pour new wine into old wineskins. If they do, the skins will burst, the wine will run out and the wineskins will be ruined."
MATTHEW 9:17

The gospel of Jesus Christ is not like a patch of denim on an old garment. Those who choose Jesus Christ, must be prepared to allow the Holy Spirit to destroy and recreate each old concept, habit, way of handling conflict, everything you are.

SEPTEMBER 14

Jesus said ... 4

"I am sending you out like sheep among wolves."
MATTHEW 10:16

Jesus conquered us with the truth. We read about the terrible suffering that Jesus predicted for us and we are not afraid. A miracle has happened to you, that God is in you, above you, around you and that you belong to him. Just as he promised.

SEPTEMBER 15

Jesus said ... 5

"The kingdom of heaven is like yeast ... "
MATTHEW 13:33

To a world of war and hatred, selfishness and immorality, a little yeast-plant is added: a plant of love, humility, self-denial, faith and suffering. Jesus predicted that something completely different will triumph over everything that is evil. "Wonderful!" the children of God rejoice. Christianity is not a spectator sport: it is being like yeast.

SEPTEMBER 16

Jesus said ... 6

"Therefore, whoever humbles himself like this child is the greatest in the kingdom of heaven."
MATTHEW 18:3

Jesus called a little one to him ... blessed child! How does this child stand there? Trusting. Without anything to offer, helpless, poor, totally dependent on his mercy, weak, without clever arguments or pretence. How do we stand there? Contemplating from a distance?

SEPTEMBER 17

Jesus said ... 7

"As it was in the days of Noah, so it will be at the coming of the Son of Man."
MATTHEW 24:37

Everyone simply has to think about the unimaginable, unexpected day when Jesus will come again. Is it essential, we ask. If we don't have this expectation we so easily neglect our relationship with the Bridegroom who will come to fetch us to be in his presence for eternity.

SEPTEMBER 18

Jesus said ... 8

"I tell you the truth, no one can enter the kingdom of God unless he is born of water and the Spirit."
JOHN 3:5

Rebirth is the invisible wind of God: the power of change which blows through me. Conversion means not fleeing from the wind, but opening up your whole being like open arms and pleading: Blow through me, oh Spirit; I am coming, Lord Jesus, I am coming.

Jesus said ... 9

"I tell you the truth, whoever hears my word and believes him who sent me has eternal life and will not be condemned."
JOHN 15:24

Do you know what despair is? It is remembering how you have lived. Jesus Christ offers to every desperate person the only way out of the most terrifying experience in heaven and on earth. Whoever obeys the command in *John 15:24* will not be condemned; he has crossed over to eternal life.

Jesus said ... 10

"Then you will know the truth, and the truth will set you free."
JOHN 8:32

We may think that the only things we should be freed of, are problems like bulimia and jealousy. But when we get to know the truth, Jesus will set us free from things that we never even regarded as chains. If you become a disciple of Jesus, the *before-* and *after-*pictures will surprise you in a few years' time.

SEPTEMBER 21

Solomon said ... 1

"The fear of the Lord is the beginning of knowledge."
PROVERBS 1:7

Maybe you are trying to hide the fact that you are a Christian. By being reticent, by denying Jesus, trying to protect yourself from raised eyebrows, you are depriving yourself of the biggest opportunity for growth. Not to mention the risk ... for Jesus says if we deny him before others, he will deny us before his Father in heaven.

Solomon said ... 2

"Trust in the Lord with all your heart ... "
PROVERBS 3:5

How many of us can stick the following house rules to our fridges? A. Nobody undertakes anything before the family has prayed about it. B. Any relationship, change of career, budget, yes everything that we do, should first be submitted to God for approval.

Solomon said ... 3

"Do not withhold good from those who deserve it ... "
PROVERBS 3:27

We can only live according to God's will by praying continually. To be able to live in peace with relatives annoying you, to be constantly filled with goodwill: can it be done? Only if you are constantly on your knees.

Solomon said ... 4

"Drink water from your own cistern ... "
PROVERBS 5:15

You who are reading here ... Are you snatching a few quick gulps from someone else's well? That man is his wife's most precious possession, you know? The Bible tells us that God sees everything. It is impossible to sin in secrecy.

Solomon said ... 5

"The memory of the righteous will be a blessing, but the name of the wicked will rot."
PROVERBS 10:7

"The man of integrity walks securely, but he who takes crooked paths will be found out."
(Proverbs 10:9)

Solomon said ... 6

"Each heart knows its own bitterness, and no one else can share its joy."
PROVERBS 14:10

Maybe you are refusing to dig out the root of bitterness. Bitterness that has taken root in your soul, will cause you to brood all day long over the full extent, the full weight of your suffering. Bitterness doesn't *belong* in you!

Solomon said ... 7

"To man belong the plans of the heart, but from the LORD comes the reply of the tongue."
PROVERBS 16:1

There was a time when God was such a reality that all expressions of human intentions were concluded with the abbreviation D.V. - God willing. How many of us take the trouble to teach this abbreviation and its meaning to our children?

Solomon said ... 8

"A perverse man stirs up dissension, and a gossip separates close friends."
PROVERBS 16:28

"What dainty morsels rumors are. They are eaten with great relish!" *(Living Bible).*

"The tongue has the power of life and death, and those who love it will eat its fruit" *(Proverbs 18:21).*

Solomon said ... 9

"Like clouds and wind without rain is a man who boasts of gifts he does not give."
PROVERBS 25:14

Until recently it was one of those things that distinguished us from worldlings: you could depend on Christians. But now things have changed. People don't buy your religion because you have broken your promise on *one* single occasion.

Solomon said ... 10

"Four things on earth are small, yet they are extremely wise: ants ... conies ... locusts ... a lizard ..."
PROVERBS 30:24-28

The small creatures that amazed the author of Proverbs didn't have any say in their being an ant or a grasshopper. *We*, however, have a choice: to be God's child, with all the beautiful characteristics of these little creatures.

OCTOBER

OCTOBER 1

Paul said ... 1

"Carry each other's burdens,
and in this way you will
fulfil the law of Christ."
GALATIANS 6:2

Is this what we do? Or do we rather not interfere when someone falls into sin? We rather discuss them with others ... and we gloat: we have so few sins.

OCTOBER 2

Paul said ... 2

... "At one time we too were foolish, disobedient, deceived and enslaved by all kinds of passions and pleasures."
TITUS 3:3

You say: "I am what I am: religion cannot change me. Leave me alone." If you are making these kind of statements, you can know for sure: you have been maimed by sin and Jesus Christ wants to change you. You *can* change for Jesus reaches out to every person who has been maimed by sin.

Paul said ... 3

"Therefore, I declare to you today that I am innocent of the blood of all men. For I have not hesitated to proclaim to you the whole will of God."
Acts 20:26, 27

Paul's words are food for thought. Where the message of redemption is being heard the responsibility to be saved or doomed is ours.

Paul said ... 4

"For you did not receive a spirit that makes you a slave again to fear, but you received the Spirit of sonship. And by him we cry, 'Abba, Father.'"
ROMANS 8:15

Those who say it is terrible to be a Christian, think that we should live like the Dachau prisoners of war. Paul says it is exactly how we shouldn't live. It is, by the way, how those live who are controlled by the devil and who are slaves of Satan. We are children and heirs!

OCTOBER 5

Paul said ... 5

"Who shall separate us from the love of Christ? Shall trouble or hardship or persecution or famine or nakedness or danger or sword?"
ROMANS 8:35

Aunty Jo: "Every time I read these verses I want to interpret them as follows: GOD AROUND ME GOD AROUND ME GOD AROUND ME GOD AROUND ME ... into all eternity."

OCTOBER 6

Paul said ... 6

"Oh, the depth of the riches of the wisdom and knowledge of God! How unsearchable his judgments and his paths beyond tracing out!"
ROMANS 11:33

Before getting married one asks: "Who is this person I'm getting married to? Who is this person with whom I will have a day-by-day, night-by-night, hour-by-hour relationship for life? Forget about Paul, David, everyone. Who is God to *you*?

OCTOBER 7

Paul said ... 7

"We who are strong ought to bear with the failings of the weak and not to please ourselves."
ROMANS 15:1

Not exactly a message for our times, we think. This isn't a decade for praise, encouragement, tolerance and goodwill. Could it be that people are so desperate, violent and unstable because the believers, you and I, have neglected our duty?

OCTOBER 8

Paul said ... 8

"And we ... are being transformed into his likeness with ever-increasing glory, which comes from the Lord, who is the Spirit."
2 CORINTHIANS 3:18

Sanctification occurs in the lives of fragile and fallible people who read their Bible, pray and obey the Word. The faces of these clay jar people begin to beam. The better we get to know Jesus, the more the jar of clay gets filled with light, joy, hope, certainty and love.

OCTOBER 9

Paul said ... 9

" ... dear friends, let us purify ourselves from everything that contaminates body and spirit ... "
2 CORINTHIANS 7:1

Being a Christian means seeing oneself as a temple. What will be inside if the doors are suddenly opened? The remnants of immoral novels and films, the flotsam of lust, the vomit of anger and bitterness, the stains of disobedience to all those instructions of God which do not suit us?

OCTOBER 10

Paul said ... 10

"Here is a trustworthy saying that deserves full acceptance: Christ Jesus came into the world to save sinners - of whom I am the worst"
1 TIMOTHY 1:15

Before us we have ... the Bible, the only plan for redemption, my hope for life and death and my plight in one paragraph. Have you already begun to consider it as important?

Isaiah had to say ... 1

"'Come now, let us reason together,' says the LORD. 'Though your sins are like scarlet, they shall be as white as snow ...'"

ISAIH 1:18

We take dreadful risks with the almighty God. But, like in the times of Isaiah, God offers his complete forgiveness to everyone who kneels before him in repentance. Our attitude towards God's undeserved offer will determine whether we will share in his blessings or not.

OCTOBER 12

Isaiah had to say ... 2

"The people walking in darkness have seen a great light ... "
ISAIAH 9:2

Jesus *has come*. He *has been* born and named ... Wonderful Counsellor ... do we seek his advice? Mighty God ... why are we then so desperate? Prince of Peace ... do we believe that he can bring divine peace into our homes? The people who lived in Isaiah's time waited and yearned. We have seen, found ... and turned away from him.

Isaiah had to say ... 3

"You boast, 'We have entered into a covenant with death, with the grave we have made an agreement. When an overwhelming scourge sweeps by, it cannot touch us ... "
ISAIAH 28:15

We live under a big illusion. We wear masks, play church, tell lies about our so-called religiousness ... But, says the Lord, D-day will come. Make very sure with whom and with what you are living.

OCTOBER 14

Isaiah had to say ... 4

"Look upon Zion, the city of our festivals; your eyes will see Jerusalem, a peaceful abode."
ISAIH 33:20

The believer will see the King in all his glory. "Look, he is coming with the clouds, and every eye will see him ... " Who are those who will live in the eternal Jerusalem? Those whose sins have been forgiven. Do you thank God for this prophecy?

Isaiah had to say ... 5

"The grass withers and the flowers fall, but the word of our God stands forever."
ISAIAH 40:8

The Bible is the eternal Word of the eternal God. This includes every promise, every warning and every prophecy. Has the implication of this occurred to you yet?

Isaiah had to say ... 6

"Who has measured the waters in the hollow of his hand, or with the breadth of his hand marked off the heavens?"
ISAIAH 40:12

Isaiah sees how the mighty God holds the mountains and oceans, nations and islands in the hollow of his hand and how he has marked off the heavens. This God says: "You are mine" *(Isaiah 43:1)*. Is the fear which we experience not the crudest form of unbelief?

OCTOBER 17

Isaiah had to say ... 7

"A bruised reed he will not break, and a smouldering wick he will not snuff out."
ISAIAH 42:3

Death itself couldn't extinguish the Flame of Life, for Jesus *is* the Flame of Life, the eternal Source of Energy behind all life, the Unshakeable who can carry, heal and control tens of thousands of bruised reeds.

OCTOBER 18

Isaiah had to say ... 8

"'You are my witnesses,' declares the LORD, 'and my servant whom I have chosen, so that you may know and believe me ...'"

ISAIAH 43:10

... So that you may know me? God desires that you and I should know him, that I, the willowy woman, whose only interests are my diet and aerobics, should meet the Creator of heaven and earth and set new goals for my life according to his plan.

OCTOBER 19

Isaiah had to say ... 9

"This is what the LORD says - your Redeemer, who formed you in the womb: I am the LORD ... "
ISAIAH 44:24

Somewhere in the big Riddle which is God, we discover a more puzzling riddle: that he who can create and destroy as he wishes is *love*, and that he cares for minute ants, gives kittens as playmates to little children, and saves his own creatures, who are corrupted by sin, through his blood.

Isaiah had to say ... 10

"I have not spoken in secret, from somewhere in a land of darkness; I have not said to Jacob's descendants, 'Seek me in vain.' I, the Lord speak the truth; I declare what is right."
ISAIAH 45:19

"Even to your old age and grey hairs I am he, I am he who will sustain you. I have made you and I will carry you; I will sustain you and I will rescue you" *(Isaiah 46:4).*

OCTOBER 21

Malachi had to say ... 1

"'I have loved you,' says the Lord. 'If I am a father, where is the honour due to me?'"
MALACHI 1:2, 6

Just like the congregation of 400 B.C. we are also guilty of bringing blind, sick and paralysed animals before the Lord as sacrifices. It is how we pray as a family, how we are involved in church activities, how we live religiously that satisfy or dissatisfy the Lord. Will he be satisfied with your way of living?

OCTOBER 22

Malachi had to say ... 2

"If you do not listen ... I will send a curse upon you ... I will spread on your faces the offal from your festival sacrifices."
MALACHI 2:2-3

God hates impious behaviour towards him and offerings given with disrespect. He demands that we should trust and obey him totally. He spells out his will and demands that we should convey it undiluted, 100% pure, to others. What kind of priest are you?

OCTOBER 23

Malachi had to say ... 3

"From (the priest's) mouth men should seek instruction - because he is the messenger of the LORD ... "
MALACHI 2:7

Many things, like organising wedding receptions or special preachers, can be done with one's Bible closed, but with a closed Bible one cannot be the Lord's messenger. One will not know God's will and will not be able to convey it to others.

Malachi had to say ... 4

"The LORD is acting as the witness between you and the wife of your youth, because you have broken faith with her ... "
MALACHI 2:14

God knows what goes on behind closed doors. He will not be mocked: if he isn't King over your marriages, we are praying in vain at public altars for peace and prosperity.

Malachi had to say ... 5

"He will purify the Levites and refine them ... Then the LORD will have men who will bring offerings in righteousness ... "
MALACHI 3:3

It has always been easy to throw things before the Lord: our fifty rand notes, our cakes for the church fête, our worn clothes for the poor. But God wants a different offering: He wants righteous deeds from a purified heart.

OCTOBER 26

Malachi had to say ... 6

"'Return to me ...' says the LORD Almighty. But you ask: 'How are we to return?'"
MALACHI 3:7

In other words: Keep it. I don't need your demanding presence in my life. But wait: God can continue to exist undisturbed from eternity to eternity, and remain silent for 400 years. It is us who die after 70 or 80 years, with every opportunity to get to know him, lost forever.

Malachi had to say ... 7

"Will a man rob God?
Yet you rob me."
MALACHI 3:8

During a plague of locusts and drought God tells his people: "Bring the whole tithe into the storehouse, that there may be food in my house." God asks the full tithe during a drought. What is he actually asking? Unconditional faith which he promises not to leave unanswered.

Malachi had to say ... 8

"You have said, 'It is futile to serve God. What did we gain by carrying out his requirements?'"
MALACHI 3:14

In Malachi 3 the implication is: Of what use is religion to us? We want to be rewarded for our devotion. Is this perhaps the intention of *your* heart?

OCTOBER 29

Malachi had to say ... 9

"A scroll of remembrance was written in his presence concerning those who feared the LORD and honoured his name."
MALACHI 3:16

We sometimes think we are merely a few women searching painstakingly for answers in God's Word, there where we are busy studying the Bible. But God sees us there. When we value his name, our names are also written down in his book of remembrance.

OCTOBER 30

Malachi had to say ... 10

"But for you who revere my name, the sun of righteousness will rise ..."
MALACHI 4:2

Is it merely interesting that the triumph of the Light over darkness, the final subjection of everything in heaven and on earth to God, the Creator and King, is discussed with uncomprehending people? What do you say after you have read the last chapter in the Old Testament?

Revelation Revealed ... 1

"Blessed is the one who reads the words of this prophecy ... and take to heart what is written in it ... "
REVELATION 1:3

The main theme of REVELATION is Jesus' triumphant victory over all his enemies. Read it attentively and take it to heart, for then you will be blessed as our text for today promises us.

NOVEMBER

Revelation Revealed ... 2

"'I am the First and the Last. I am the Living One.'"
REVELATION 1:17, 18

Jesus reveals himself in a symbolic way to John: he is no longer the same humiliated Jesus of the cross; the trumpet sound of his voice means that he is speaking with authority. "I now rule in heaven, John," is actually what Jesus is saying. "But I also walk amongst your congregations and churches, for they are mine."

Revelation Revealed ... 3

"I know your deeds, your hard work ... Yet I hold this against you ... "
REVELATION 2:2, 4

In Revelation we read how Jesus walks among the churches. What is the situation in your church? Are you perhaps Ephesus, the hive of activity where the love for Jesus has grown cold? Or Sardis: the church which hardly breathes? Or Laodicea, the fool's paradise?

NOVEMBER 3

Revelation Revealed ... 4

"'To him who sits on the throne and to the Lamb be praise and honour and glory and power ... '"
REVELATION 5:13

John is summoned to the control room of the universe. The centre of the control room is he who sits on the throne. Finally the universe realizes: *He is Lord!* Therefore the church sings the song in *Revelation 5:9-14*. Read it aloud today and join in their song.

Revelation Revealed ... 5

"When he opened the fifth seal, I saw ... the souls of those ... slain because of the ... testimony they had maintained."
REVELATION 6:9

Revelation 6:1 - 8:1 contains images of the church in the world. There will be victory, but also conflict, struggle, war and prosecution, etc. Jesus has already shown us everything. Nothing is out of control - God doesn't sleep.

NOVEMBER 5

Revelation

Revealed ... 6

"Then I heard the number of those who were sealed: 144, 000 from all the tribes of Israel."
REVELATION 7:4

Your problem is not to know *how many* believers are in heaven: you should ask how they got there. Did they try hard? The answer: " ... they have washed their robes and made them white in the blood of the Lamb. Therefore, they are before the throne of God ... "

NOVEMBER 6

Revelation Revealed ... 7

"And I saw the seven angels ... and to them were given seven trumpets."
REVELATION 8:2

The compassionate and gracious God warns the world: Repent! This time we hear the blast of trumpets: it is like powerful and dramatic music of all the many ways in which God wants to save the people on earth. Seven trumpets warn: the hour of judgement is coming. Turn to the Lord!

NOVEMBER 7

Revelation Revealed ... 8

"The dragon gave the beast his ... great authority."
REVELATION 13:2

Satan summons two monstrous helpers: First there is the beast out of the sea *(Rev. 13:1-10), the world powers.* This predicts that we will be governed by *Anti-Christian* governments. Then the beast out of the earth *(Rev. 13:11-18), false religion,* false ideologies. This is what our world looks like. Unsafe? Oh, how we need God!

Revelation Revealed ... 9

"And ... my two witnesses ... will prophesy ... , clothed in sackcloth."
REVELATION 11:3

The offspring of the woman are loyal individuals, *two witnesses.* These actors aren't given easy roles: they will be killed and their bodies will lie in the streets. They are promised the triumphant resurrection and eternal joy with God. They accept this role. Are you one of these witnesses?

NOVEMBER 9

Revelation Revealed ... 10

"Blessed are those who wash their robes, that they may ... go through the gates into the city."
REVELATION 22:14

Do you now realise how we would have been drifting about between somewhere and nowhere if the book REVELATION hadn't been in the Bible? How confused, how shocked we would have been by all the disasters? How we even would have questioned our earthly purpose?

NOVEMBER 10

Eternal Promise 1

"For God so loved the world that he gave his one and only Son, that whoever believes in him shall not perish but have eternal life. For God did not send his Son into the world to condemn the world, but to save the world through him."

JOHN 3:16, 17

What do I lose if I don't embrace this promise?

NOVEMBER 11

Eternal Promise 2

"Peter replied, 'Repent and be baptized, every one of you, in the name of Jesus Christ for the forgiveness of your sins. And you will receive the gift of the Holy Spirit.'"
ACTS 2:38, 39

"'The promise is for you and your children and for all who are far off - for all whom the Lord our God will call.'" (Acts 2:39).

Eternal Promise 3

"I warn everyone who hears the words of the prophecy of this book: If anyone adds anything to them, God will add to him the plagues described in this book. And if anyone takes words away from this book of prophecy, God will take away from him his share in the tree of life and in the holy city, which are described in this book. He who testifies to these things says, 'Yes, I am coming soon.'"

REVELATION 22:18-20

Eternal Promise 4

"... But showing love to a thousand generations of those who love me and keep my commandments."
EXODUS 20:6

If you do not confess your sins, your children *will* bear the consequences. If you love the Lord, your children will, like those of all believers, enjoy the glorious life-long joy of his blessings.

NOVEMBER 14

Eternal Promise 5

*"I tell you, whoever ack-
nowledges me before men,
the Son of Man will also
acknowledge him before
the angels of God. But he
who disowns me before men
will be disowned before
the angels of God."*

LUKE 12:8, 9

NOVEMBER 15

Eternal Promise 6

"All that the Father gives me will come to me and whoever comes to me I will never drive away."

JOHN 6:37

For which age is this promise intended? For people of all times. People of the Middle Ages could accept it. Teenagers in the year 2000 may embrace it. It is intended for the hottest hour of the day and the darkest hour of the night, following the biggest sin in your life.

NOVEMBER 16

Eternal Promise 7

"For the trumpet will sound, the dead will be raised imperishable ... Death has been swallowed up in victory. Where, O death, is your victory?"
1 CORINTHIANS 15:52, 54, 55

John Donne called out: "Death, be not proud, though some have called thee mighty and dreadful, for thou art not so; One short sleep past, we wake eternally ... "

NOVEMBER 17

Eternal Promise 8

"But seek first his kingdom and his righteousness, and all these things will be given to you as well."
MATTHEW 6:33

If I were to believe this promise, my whole value system would change. The earthly treasure-chest of someone who leaves his daily needs in God's hands and who seeks God's kingdom, lies open. The few rands that might be lost, is not the end of the world any longer.

Eternal Promise 9

"And if anyone gives even a cup of cold water to one of these little ones because he is my disciple, I tell you the truth, he will certainly not lose his reward."
MATTHEW 10:42

True charitable deeds are done to honour God, in gratitude towards him. We do it for him: it is a matter between him and us. "How can I repay the Lord for all his goodness to me?" *(Psalm 116:12)*.

NOVEMBER 19

Eternal Promise 10

"Do not let your hearts be troubled. Trust in God; trust also in me. In my Father's house are many rooms; if it were not so, I would have told you. I am going there to prepare a place for you, I will come back and take you to be with me that you may also be where I am."

JOHN 14:1-3

NOVEMBER 20

Command 1

"'Leave your country ... and go to the land I will show you. ... and all peoples on earth will be blessed through you.'"
GENESIS 12:1, 3

An adventure with God was waiting for Abram. What would have happened if he hadn't obeyed? Because he was obedient, all the nations of the world are blessed: the Messiah descended from him. When God calls us ... who knows what could happen!

NOVEMBER 21

Command 2

"Go to ... Nineveh and proclaim to it the message I give you."
JONAH 3:2

Suppose God says to you: Go to X and preach the Word of the Lord to those people. They could represent a hated government or be the strikers who gave you sleepless nights ... God sent Jonah to the worst of the worst, to his enemies. God can give his mercy to any person, whether we like him or not. Will you co-operate with God?

Command No. 3

"So now, go. I am sending you to Pharaoh to bring my people ... out of Egypt."
EXODUS 3:10

Dealing with God is a matter of faith, not of emotion. Moses' reality was a land filled with slaves. God's reality, on the contrary, was a new land filled with free people. Suppose Moses didn't believe the seemingly impossible? What is your reality? And what is your impossible command?

NOVEMBER 23

Command 4

"'Go! This man is my chosen instrument to carry my name before the Gentiles ... '"
ACTS 9:15

When God comes to stand before us like he stood before Paul on the road to Damascus, he offers us forgiveness. But this is only the beginning, the first moment. Then follows the development of our true potential, talents, abilities and gifts. He gives us the power to have courage, to persevere and to be noble.

NOVEMBER 24

Command 5

"'... I have never eaten anything impure or unclean.'"
ACTS 10:14

Peter has serious doubts about the people to whom God sends him. He doesn't socialise with them. He calls out: "But I have never!" It is a poor excuse before God. When God commands us, the excuse: 'I have never', is no longer valid.

NOVEMBER 25

Command 6

*"Go south to the road ...
that goes down from
Jerusalem to Gaza."*
ACTS 8:26

God has no favourites *(Titus 2:11)*. Whether we like it or not. Philip who was filled with the Holy Spirit, liked it and explained the gospel to this unusual character who was precious in God's eyes. This poor outcast who couldn't enter the inner court of the temple in the past, knew eternal joy for the very first time! Will *you* go, Philippa?

Command 7

"The Lord said to him, 'Go back the way you came, and go to the Desert of Damascus.'"
1 KINGS 19:1-15

God has two instructions for Elijah: "Get up and eat, for the journey is too much for you." The journey? Elijah was hoping to die. But God knows all about our worst times; he is there when we foolishly choose rather to die than to live. The second instruction follows later: "Go back the way you came."

NOVEMBER 27

Command 8

"You must go to everyone I send you to and say whatever I command you."
JEREMIAH 1:7

If Jeremiah had to choose a pair of soul mates, it would have been Moses and Isaiah. All three of them have said to the Lord: "I do not know how to speak." God replied: "You must go to everyone I send you to ... Do not be afraid of them, for I am with you and will rescue you." Have you allowed God to touch *your* mouth?

Command 9

"I will betroth you to me forever; I will betroth you in righteousness and justice, in love and compassion. I will betroth you in faithfulness, and you will acknowledge the LORD … I will say to those called 'not my people,' 'You are my people'; and they will say, 'You are my God.'"

HOSEA 2:19, 20, 23

Is this drama perhaps being staged for you?

NOVEMBER 29

Command 10

"'I have brought you glory on earth by completing the work you gave me to do.'"
JOHN 17:4

The Son of God respects the Father so much that he doesn't change his instructions at all. He knows there is only one truth, the truth of God. And we? We regard God's instructions as unimportant. We think we can be more daring than the Son of God. We believe we can ridicule, ignore, twist and forget God's instructions.

NOVEMBER 30

God of the Old Testament 1

" ... and the Spirit of God was hovering over the waters."
GENESIS 1:2

God is the great Mystery who had soared aloft the dark deep waters before creation. We hear him say: "Let us make man in our image ... and let them rule ... over all the earth, ... And suddenly we are also something - representatives of the great Unknown, the Eternal One.

DECEMBER

God of the Old Testament 2

"God said to Moses, 'I am who I am.'"
EXODUS 3:14

The God of the universe wants to be in contact with his creatures. You and I know *with certainty and joy* that this God is the true God: the God who is greater than the thoughts of the wisest man; the God who reveals himself as triumphant, mighty and perfect, and mercifully miraculously obscures himself as the unassailable I AM.

DECEMBER 2

God of the Old Testament 3

"'I am the Lord your God, ... You shall have not other gods before me."
EXODUS 20:2, 3

When God gives us the Ten Commandments, we see the ten masterly strokes with which the Master controls our thoughts, society, family life, our spiritual and physical health, our possessions and our legal system. It gives glory to his Name, his Being, his church and the Sabbath.

DECEMBER 3

God of the Old Testament 4

"... 'I am going to come to you in a dense cloud ... '"
EXODUS 19:9

Who can prevent the sound of the heavenly trumpets and God's commands? Who can control an earthquake, touch a burning mountain and silence the burst of thunder? God IS God, the signs of his appearance proclaim. I AM WHO I AM: *the enormous enigma*, the totally Other, the One and Only.

God of the Old Testament 5

"The Lord would speak to Moses face to face, as a man speaks with his friend."
EXODUS 33:11

Despite Moses' many faults (he has committed murder, to name but one), God regards him as his friend, for Moses trusts his Friend, asks his advice and speaks to him constantly. God is a wonderful Friend to those who want Him as a friend. This friendship is meant for you too.

DECEMBER 5

God of the Old Testament 6

"Then the Lord ... proclaimed his name, the LORD."
EXODUS 34:5

God gives Moses the meaning of his name: the compassionate and gracious God, slow to anger, abounding in love and faithfulness, maintaining love to thousands, and forgiving wickedness and sin. Yet he does not leave the guilty unpunished; he punishes the father's sins in the sons and grandsons and even later generations.

DECEMBER 6

God of the Old Testament 7

"Speak to the entire assembly of Israel and say to them: ... "
LEVITICUS 19:2

When God speaks to the church, he speaks to the entire congregation. Every remark such as: "She always pretends to be holy ... " crumbles before God's Word. Those who stand before God and confess that they know him, are without exception being called upon to be holy.

DECEMBER 7

God of the Old Testament 8

" ... Be careful not to carry a load on the Sabbath day ... , but keep the Sabbath day holy, ..."
JEREMIAH 17:21, 22

Our spiritual temperature can be measured by our reaction to the fourth commandment. God instructed that his day, the Sabbath, should be a day of seclusion, service, worship and prayer. The way you keep the Sabbath gives an indication of how serious you are about God.

DECEMBER 8

God of the Old Testament 9

"Like the appearance of a rainbow in the clouds on a rainy day, so was the radiance around him."
EZEKIEL 1:28

God addressed Ezekiel as "Son of dust". It is only through the Holy Spirit that a being of dust can stand erect before the great Inconceivable. Kneel, son of dust, until the Spirit gives you the strength to stand before God.

DECEMBER 9

God of the Old Testament 10

" ... Bethlehem ... out of you will come ... (a) ruler ... whose origins are from of old ... "
MICAH 5:1

This promise to Bethlehem in the year 500 B.C. is fulfilled in the person of Jesus Christ. One promise, however, remains unfulfilled before the name of God will finally be confessed by every tongue: the second coming of Christ *(Acts 1:11)*. What makes you think that God will not fulfil it too?

God with us 1

"Do not be afraid. I bring you good news of great joy that will be for all the people."
LUKE 2:10, 11

In that wonderful night the sound of joy echoes on earth: the promises of God, the Unknowable, have been fulfilled. God is here. God is with mankind on earth.

DECEMBER 11

God with us 2

"'Ha! What do you want with us, Jesus of Nazareth?'"
LUKE 4:34

The devil in the demon-possessed man from Capernaum echoes our resistance: do we want to be delivered of those things that have been fun, normal and reasonably to us? Suddenly we realise: *we* are the poor, the prisoners, the blind, the oppressed. It is *we* who should shed tears of gratitude over the Lord's year of mercy.

God with us 3

"'Put out into deep water, and let down the nets for a catch.' ... 'Don't be afraid, from now on you will catch men.'"
LUKE 5:4, 10

Disciples of the Lord are given many different tools: fishing-nets, typewriters, guitars, pens, spades, rakes, paintbrushes ... but the instruction remains the same: "From now on you will catch men."

DECEMBER 13

God with us 4

"Then he went up and touched the coffin ... He said, 'Young man, I say to you, get up!'"
LUKE 7:14

Madam, are you sure your child isn't dead? Ephesians 2:1, 4, 5: "But because of his great love for us, God who is rich in mercy, made us alive with Christ even when we were dead in transgressions." Stand still next to the bier. He who conquers death is here.

DECEMBER 14

God with us 5

" ... she began to wet his feet with her tears. Then she wiped them with her hair, kissed them and poured perfume over them."
LUKE 7:37, 38

Jesus looks at the scarlet woman. And he demonstrates: I have come to the world for the likes of her. Jesus tells her: "Your sins are forgiven." He has nothing to say to the onlooking Pharisees nor to the modern-day ladies who are virtuous in their own eyes.

DECEMBER 15

God with us 6

" ... a woman ... had been subject to bleeding ... , but no one could heal her."
LUKE 8:43

Haemorrhage is an unmentionable ailment. What about other secret, foul ailments which cannot be removed by surgical knife like bitterness, lovelessness, etc.? "These are not dirty ailments," we protest. But they are! They are so dirty and deadly that they cannot be cured by a doctor. Except by the Visiting Healer.

DECEMBER 16

God with us 7

"We have only five loafs of bread and two fish ... "
LUKE 9:13

Suddenly the disciples realise that they need Jesus to do the impossible through them. They take the bread and fish which he keeps on breaking and breaking and making more and more, and they learn: all the glory belongs to him. We are merely his helpers, his servants. Nothing of this is our due: a moment ago we were mere helpless onlookers.

DECEMBER 17

God with us 8

"'Martha, Martha,' the Lord answered, '... only one thing is needed.'"
LUKE 10:41, 42

Jesus never criticised kitchen work. He only disapproves of a schedule which doesn't include Him. There are thousands of women like Martha who forfeit fellowship with Jesus because they choose the fluff on the carpet and ants in the sugar-bowl.

DECEMBER 18

God with us 9

"So I say to you: Ask and it will be given to you ... "
LUKE 11:9

Suppose you have to make a list today of the things you would seek and ask for, knock for on God's door in the middle of the night - what will it be? A companion for life? Yes, if you are a family person. The Holy Spirit? Oh yes, yes! Deliverance from sin? Yes, a thousand times yes! This is the good news: seek, ask, knock. It is the Father who opens the door.

DECEMBER 19

God with us 10

"Jesus ... went out and asked them, 'Who is it you want?' 'Jesus of Nazareth', they replied. 'I am he', Jesus said."
JOHN 18:4, 5

Jesus came forward in Gethsemane to remove the burdens from your shoulders, to take all the self-reproach of your heart on him. He who steps forward there in Gethsemane, is *God* who came to die for creatures who are squirming in the mud, the Potter who came to die for the sherd.

DECEMBER 20

God in us 1

*"Because you are sons,
God sent the Spirit of his
Son into our hearts ... "*
GALATIANS 4:6, 7

The Spirit who had once soared aloft the deep waters, has found a new home in you and me. *Child of God!* calls the jubilant Spirit in us. And as if something wonderful is the most natural thing on earth, we accept the fact that we are descendants of Abraham *(Gen. 12:3)*. Blessed ... has anybody ever been more blessed than you?

DECEMBER 21

God in us 2

"And you also were included in Christ when you heard the word of truth, the gospel of your salvation."
EPHESIANS 1:13

"His presence within us is God's guarantee that he really will give us all that he promised; and the Spirit's seal upon us means that God has already purchased us and that he guarantees to bring us to himself" *(Living Bible)*.

DECEMBER 22

God in us 3

"I pray also that the eyes of your heart may be enlightened in order that you may know the hope to which he has called you."
EPHESIANS 1:18

Paul prays that we may begin to understand who is living in us and what his presence means in our daily lives. Without this understanding, we will be stumbling along in our own strength, while the power sources of heaven are at our disposal.

DECEMBER 23

God in us 4

" ... you must no longer live as the Gentiles do ... separated from the life of God ... "
EPHESIANS 4:17, 18

In every person's life there is a *before* and a *now*. Blessed is the person whose *before* is empty and whose *now* is full: full of joy and lasting hope and full of God and thoughts of God. Paul says: "You were taught to be made new in the attitude of your minds, and to put on the new self, created to be like God."

God in us 5

" ... Live as children of light (for the fruit of the light consists in all goodness, righteousness and truth) ... "
EPHESIANS 5:8, 9

We have the responsibility to co-operate with the Holy Spirit towards our own sanctification. "Find out what pleases the Lord," says Paul. This means deliberately taking the Spirit of God into account constantly. Is my smoking acceptable to you, indwelling Holy Spirit? Is it all right with you that I ... ?

God in us 6

"Be strong in the Lord ... Put on the full armour of God so that you can take your stand against the devil's schemes."
EPHESIANS 6:10,11

Dear Mother, even if your son only learns to wear his uniform properly, to hold his rifle correctly and to have the correct posture for attack and defence, every second which he spends in the Defence Force, is worth while. I *must* learn spiritual control. It is my blueprint for survival.

DECEMBER 26

God in us 7

" ... so that you may become blameless and pure ... "
PHILIPPIANS 2:15

It is very difficult to be a child of the light and a light-bearer when your spouse has walked out on you or if your employer has given you a golden handshake. However, says the Word, this is how a believer should behave. Degenerate and corrupt people watch us through narrowed eyes to see if the light is still light.

DECEMBER 27

God in us 8

"Do not cast me from your presence or take your Holy Spirit from me."
PSALM 51:11

Finally, after he has disobeyed every commandment in the book, David knows what God expects from him: "Surely you desire truth in the inner parts." Is that how you will conclude this year?

DECEMBER 28

God in us 9

"For if you live according to the sinful nature, you will die ... "
ROMANS 8:13

The mighty power of the Holy Spirit can destroy our sinful nature like an eggshell. If we leave this energy field, that same sinful nature can become a steel coffin from which we cannot escape.

DECEMBER 29

God in us 10

*"Never be lacking in zeal,
but keep your spiritual
fervour, serving the Lord."*
ROMANS 12:11

The total revolution in our lives for the sake of which the Son of God died on the cross, comes from God; the desire for change comes from the Holy Spirit. *Romans 12:9-21* teaches us how we should co-operate with God so that *our* lives can improve.

Here Stands a Woman With a Flag

"For the kingdom of God is not a matter of eating and drinking, but of righteousness, peace and joy in the Holy Spirit ... "
ROMANS 14:17

The kingdom of God should be visible in every Christian woman's home. We should plant flag-poles and hoist flags: This house belongs to the Lord. The atmosphere belongs to him. This woman works for him to create this atmosphere. What is written on your flag?

God has the Last Word

"Behold, I am coming soon! My reward is with me, and I will give to everyone according to what he has done."
REVELATION 22:12

Life never ends, my friend. Therefore it will be wise to look towards eternity on this fragile, ephemeral day in December. It will be foolish, yes crazy, to ignore the outstretched hand of the Creator of eternity.

POUVOIR to be able to

IMPERFECT
je pouvais
tu pouvais
il pouvait
nous pouvions
vous pouviez
ils pouvaient

FUTURE
je pourrai
tu pourras
il pourra
nous pourrons
vous pourrez
ils pourront

PERFECT
j'ai pu
tu as pu
il a pu
nous avons pu
vous avez pu
ils ont pu

PLUPERFECT
j'avais pu
tu avais pu
il avait pu
nous avions pu
vous aviez pu
ils avaient pu

FUTURE PERFECT
j'aurai pu etc

CONDITIONAL

PRESENT
je pourrais
tu pourrais
il pourrait
nous pourrions
vous pourriez
ils pourraient

PAST
j'aurais pu
tu aurais pu
il aurait pu
nous aurions pu
vous auriez pu
ils auraient pu

SUBJUNCTIVE

IMPERFECT
je pusse
tu pusses
il pût
nous pussions
vous pussiez
ils pussent

PERFECT
j'aie pu
tu aies pu
il ait pu
nous ayons pu
vous ayez pu
ils aient pu

PARTICIPLE

PRESENT
pouvant

PAST
pu

POSSÉDER to own

PRESENT
je possède
tu possèdes
il possède
nous possédons
vous possédez
ils possèdent

IMPERFECT
je possédais
tu possédais
il possédait
nous possédions
vous possédiez
ils possédaient

FUTURE
je posséderai
tu posséderas
il possédera
nous posséderons
vous posséderez
ils posséderont

PAST HISTORIC
je possédai
tu possédas
il posséda
nous possédâmes
vous possédâtes
ils possédèrent

PERFECT
j'ai possédé
tu as possédé
il a possédé
nous avons possédé
vous avez possédé
ils ont possédé

PLUPERFECT
j'avais possédé
tu avais possédé
il avait possédé
nous avions possédé
vous aviez possédé
ils avaient possédé

PAST ANTERIOR
j'eus possédé etc

FUTURE PERFECT
j'aurai possédé etc

IMPERATIVE
possède
possédons
possédez

CONDITIONAL

PRESENT
je posséderais
tu posséderais
il posséderait
nous posséderions
vous posséderiez
ils posséderaient

PAST
j'aurais possédé
tu aurais possédé
il aurait possédé
nous aurions possédé
vous auriez possédé
ils auraient possédé

SUBJUNCTIVE

PRESENT
je possède
tu possèdes
il possède
nous possédions
vous possédiez
ils possèdent

IMPERFECT
je possédasse
tu possédasses
il possédât
nous possédassions
vous possédassiez
ils possédassent

PERFECT
j'aie possédé
tu aies possédé
il ait possédé
nous ayons possédé
vous ayez possédé
ils aient possédé

INFINITIVE

PRESENT
posséder

PAST
avoir possédé

PARTICIPLE

PRESENT
possédant

PAST
possédé

POURVOIR to provide

PRESENT	IMPERFECT	FUTURE
je pourvois	je pourvoyais	je pourvoirai
tu pourvois	tu pourvoyais	tu pourvoiras
il pourvoit	il pourvoyait	il pourvoira
nous pourvoyons	nous pourvoyions	nous pourvoirons
vous pourvoyez	vous pourvoyiez	vous pourvoirez
ils pourvoient	ils pourvoyaient	ils pourvoiront
PAST HISTORIC	**PERFECT**	**PLUPERFECT**
je pourvus	j'ai pourvu	j'avais pourvu
tu pourvus	tu as pourvu	tu avais pourvu
il pourvut	il a pourvu	il avait pourvu
nous pourvûmes	nous avons pourvu	nous avions pourvu
vous pourvûtes	vous avez pourvu	vous aviez pourvu
ils pourvurent	ils ont pourvu	ils avaient pourvu
PAST ANTERIOR	**FUTURE PERFECT**	
j'eus pourvu etc	j'aurai pourvu etc	

IMPERATIVE	CONDITIONAL PRESENT	CONDITIONAL PAST
	je pourvoirais	j'aurais pourvu
pourvois	tu pourvoirais	tu aurais pourvu
pourvoyons	il pourvoirait	il aurait pourvu
pourvoyez	nous pourvoirions	nous aurions pourvu
	vous pourvoiriez	vous auriez pourvu
	ils pourvoiraient	ils auraient pourvu

SUBJUNCTIVE

PRESENT	IMPERFECT	PERFECT
je pourvoie	je pourvusse	j'aie pourvu
tu pourvoies	tu pourvusses	tu aies pourvu
il pourvoie	il pourvût	il ait pourvu
nous pourvoyions	nous pourvussions	nous ayons pourvu
vous pourvoyiez	vous pourvussiez	vous ayez pourvu
ils pourvoient	ils pourvussent	ils aient pourvu

INFINITIVE	PARTICIPLE
PRESENT	**PRESENT**
pourvoir	pourvoyant
PAST	**PAST**
avoir pourvu	pourvu

POUSSER to push

PRESENT	IMPER
je pousse	je pouss
tu pousses	tu pouss
il pousse	il pouss
nous poussons	nous po
vous poussez	vous po
ils poussent	ils pouss
PAST HISTORIC	**PERFE**
je poussai	j'ai pous
tu poussas	tu as po
il poussa	il a pous
nous poussâmes	nous av
vous poussâtes	vous av
ils poussèrent	ils ont p
PAST ANTERIOR	**FUTUI**
j'eus poussé etc	j'aurai p

IMPERATIVE	PRESE
	je pouss
pousse	tu pouss
poussons	il pouss
poussez	nous po
	vous po
	ils pouss

SUBJU

PRESENT	IMPER
je pousse	je pouss
tu pousses	tu pouss
il pousse	il pouss
nous poussions	nous po
vous poussiez	vous po
ils poussent	ils pouss

INFINITIVE	PARTI
PRESENT	**PRESE**
pousser	poussar
PAST	**PAST**
avoir poussé	poussé

PRESENT
je peux
tu peux
il peut
nous pouvons
vous pouvez
ils peuvent
PAST HISTORIC
je pus
tu pus
il put
nous pûmes
vous pûtes
ils purent
PAST ANTERIOR
j'eus pu etc

IMPERATIVE

PRESENT
je puisse
tu puisses
il puisse
nous puissions
vous puissiez
ils puissent

INFINITIVE
PRESENT
pouvoir
PAST
avoir pu

PRESENT	IMPERFECT	FUTURE
je préfère	je préférais	je préférerai
tu préfères	tu préférais	tu préféreras
il préfère	il préférait	il préférera
nous préférons	nous préférions	nous préférerons
vous préférez	vous préfériez	vous préférerez
ils préfèrent	ils préféraient	ils préféreront
PAST HISTORIC	**PERFECT**	**PLUPERFECT**
je préférai	j'ai préféré	j'avais préféré
tu préféras	tu as préféré	tu avais préféré
il préféra	il a préféré	il avait préféré
nous préférâmes	nous avons préféré	nous avions préféré
vous préférâtes	vous avez préféré	vous aviez préféré
ils préférèrent	ils ont préféré	ils avaient préféré
PAST ANTERIOR	**FUTURE PERFECT**	
j'eus préféré etc	j'aurai préféré etc	

IMPERATIVE	CONDITIONAL	
	PRESENT	**PAST**
préfère	je préférerais	j'aurais préféré
préférons	tu préférerais	tu aurais préféré
préférez	il préférerait	il aurait préféré
	nous préférerions	nous aurions préféré
	vous préféreriez	vous auriez préféré
	ils préféreraient	ils auraient préféré

	SUBJUNCTIVE	
PRESENT	**IMPERFECT**	**PERFECT**
je préfère	je préférasse	j'aie préféré
tu préfères	tu préférasses	tu aies préféré
il préfère	il préférât	il ait préféré
nous préférions	nous préférassions	nous ayons préféré
vous préfériez	vous préférassiez	vous ayez préféré
ils préfèrent	ils préférassent	ils aient préféré

INFINITIVE	PARTICIPLE
PRESENT	**PRESENT**
préférer	préférant
PAST	**PAST**
avoir préféré	préféré

PRESENT	IMPERFECT	FUTURE
je prends	je prenais	je prendrai
tu prends	tu prenais	tu prendras
il prend	il prenait	il prendra
nous prenons	nous prenions	nous prendrons
vous prenez	vous preniez	vous prendrez
ils prennent	ils prenaient	ils prendront
PAST HISTORIC	**PERFECT**	**PLUPERFECT**
je pris	j'ai pris	j'avais pris
tu pris	tu as pris	tu avais pris
il prit	il a pris	il avait pris
nous prîmes	nous avons pris	nous avions pris
vous prîtes	vous avez pris	vous aviez pris
ils prirent	ils ont pris	ils avaient pris
PAST ANTERIOR	**FUTURE PERFECT**	
j'eus pris etc	j'aurai pris etc	

IMPERATIVE	CONDITIONAL	
	PRESENT	**PAST**
prends	je prendrais	j'aurais pris
prenons	tu prendrais	tu aurais pris
prenez	il prendrait	il aurait pris
	nous prendrions	nous aurions pris
	vous prendriez	vous auriez pris
	ils prendraient	ils auraient pris

	SUBJUNCTIVE	
PRESENT	**IMPERFECT**	**PERFECT**
je prenne	je prisse	j'aie pris
tu prennes	tu prisses	tu aies pris
il prenne	il prît	il ait pris
nous prenions	nous prissions	nous ayons pris
vous preniez	vous prissiez	vous ayez pris
ils prennent	ils prissent	ils aient pris

INFINITIVE	PARTICIPLE
PRESENT	**PRESENT**
prendre	prenant
PAST	**PAST**
avoir pris	pris

PRESENT	IMPERFECT	FUTURE
je prévaux	je prévalais	je prévaudrai
tu prévaux	tu prévalais	tu prévaudras
il prévaut	il prévalait	il prévaudra
nous prévalons	nous prévalions	nous prévaudrons
vous prévalez	vous prévaliez	vous prévaudrez
ils prévalent	ils prévalaient	ils prévaudront
PAST HISTORIC	**PERFECT**	**PLUPERFECT**
je prévalus	j'ai prévalu	j'avais prévalu
tu prévalus	tu as prévalu	tu avais prévalu
il prévalut	il a prévalu	il avait prévalu
nous prévalûmes	nous avons prévalu	nous avions prévalu
vous prévalûtes	vous avez prévalu	vous aviez prévalu
ils prévalurent	ils ont prévalu	ils avaient prévalu
PAST ANTERIOR	**FUTURE PERFECT**	
j'eus prévalu etc	j'aurai prévalu etc	

IMPERATIVE	CONDITIONAL	
	PRESENT	**PAST**
prévaux	je prévaudrais	j'aurais prévalu
prévalons	tu prévaudrais	tu aurais prévalu
prévalez	il prévaudrait	il aurait prévalu
	nous prévaudrions	nous aurions prévalu
	vous prévaudriez	vous auriez prévalu
	ils prévaudraient	ils auraient prévalu

	SUBJUNCTIVE	
PRESENT	**IMPERFECT**	**PERFECT**
je prévale	je prévalusse	j'aie prévalu
tu prévales	tu prévalusses	tu aies prévalu
il prévale	il prévalût	il ait prévalu
nous prévalions	nous prévalussions	nous ayons prévalu
vous prévaliez	vous prévalussiez	vous ayez prévalu
ils prévalent	ils prévalussent	ils aient prévalu

INFINITIVE	PARTICIPLE
PRESENT	**PRESENT**
prévaloir	prévalant
PAST	**PAST**
avoir prévalu	prévalu

PRESENT	IMPERFECT	FUTURE
je préviens	je prévenais	je préviendrai
tu préviens	tu prévenais	tu préviendras
il prévient	il prévenait	il préviendra
nous prévenons	nous prévenions	nous préviendrons
vous prévenez	vous préveniez	vous préviendrez
ils préviennent	ils prévenaient	ils préviendront
PAST HISTORIC	**PERFECT**	**PLUPERFECT**
je prévins	j'ai prévenu	j'avais prévenu
tu prévins	tu as prévenu	tu avais prévenu
il prévint	il a prévenu	il avait prévenu
nous prévînmes	nous avons prévenu	nous avions prévenu
vous prévîntes	vous avez prévenu	vous aviez prévenu
ils prévinrent	ils ont prévenu	ils avaient prévenu
PAST ANTERIOR	**FUTURE PERFECT**	
j'eus prévenu etc	j'aurai prévenu etc	

IMPERATIVE	CONDITIONAL PRESENT	CONDITIONAL PAST
préviens	je préviendrais	j'aurais prévenu
prévenons	tu préviendrais	tu aurais prévenu
prévenez	il préviendrait	il aurait prévenu
	nous préviendrions	nous aurions prévenu
	vous préviendriez	vous auriez prévenu
	ils préviendraient	ils auraient prévenu

SUBJUNCTIVE

PRESENT	IMPERFECT	PERFECT
je prévienne	je prévinsse	j'aie prévenu
tu préviennes	tu prévinsses	tu aies prévenu
il prévienne	il prévînt	il ait prévenu
nous prévenions	nous prévinssions	nous ayons prévenu
vous préveniez	vous prévinssiez	vous ayez prévenu
ils préviennent	ils prévinssent	ils aient prévenu

INFINITIVE	PARTICIPLE	NOTE
PRESENT	**PRESENT**	**convenir** takes the auxiliary 'être' when it means 'to agree'
prévenir	prévenant	
PAST	**PAST**	
avoir prévenu	prévenu	

PRÉVOIR to foresee

PRESENT	IMPERFECT	FUTURE
je prévois	je prévoyais	je prévoirai
tu prévois	tu prévoyais	tu prévoiras
il prévoit	il prévoyait	il prévoira
nous prévoyons	nous prévoyions	nous prévoirons
vous prévoyez	vous prévoyiez	vous prévoirez
ils prévoient	ils prévoyaient	ils prévoiront
PAST HISTORIC	**PERFECT**	**PLUPERFECT**
je prévis	j'ai prévu	j'avais prévu
tu prévis	tu as prévu	tu avais prévu
il prévit	il a prévu	il avait prévu
nous prévîmes	nous avons prévu	nous avions prévu
vous prévîtes	vous avez prévu	vous aviez prévu
ils prévirent	ils ont prévu	ils avaient prévu
PAST ANTERIOR	**FUTURE PERFECT**	
j'eus prévu etc	j'aurai prévu etc	

IMPERATIVE	CONDITIONAL PRESENT	CONDITIONAL PAST
	je prévoirais	j'aurais prévu
prévois	tu prévoirais	tu aurais prévu
prévoyons	il prévoirait	il aurait prévu
prévoyez	nous prévoirions	nous aurions prévu
	vous prévoiriez	vous auriez prévu
	ils prévoiraient	ils auraient prévu

SUBJUNCTIVE

PRESENT	IMPERFECT	PERFECT
je prévoie	je prévisse	j'aie prévu
tu prévoies	tu prévisses	tu aies prévu
il prévoie	il prévît	il ait prévu
nous prévoyions	nous prévissions	nous ayons prévu
vous prévoyiez	vous prévissiez	vous ayez prévu
ils prévoient	ils prévissent	ils aient prévu

INFINITIVE	PARTICIPLE
PRESENT	**PRESENT**
prévoir	prévoyant
PAST	**PAST**
avoir prévu	prévu

PROMETTRE to promise

PRESENT	IMPERFECT	FUTURE
je promets	je promettais	je promettrai
tu promets	tu promettais	tu promettras
il promet	il promettait	il promettra
nous promettons	nous promettions	nous promettrons
vous promettez	vous promettiez	vous promettrez
ils promettent	ils promettaient	ils promettront

PAST HISTORIC	PERFECT	PLUPERFECT
je promis	j'ai promis	j'avais promis
tu promis	tu as promis	tu avais promis
il promit	il a promis	il avait promis
nous promîmes	nous avons promis	nous avions promis
vous promîtes	vous avez promis	vous aviez promis
ils promirent	ils ont promis	ils avaient promis

PAST ANTERIOR	FUTURE PERFECT
j'eus promis etc	j'aurai promis etc

IMPERATIVE	CONDITIONAL	
	PRESENT	PAST
promets	je promettrais	j'aurais promis
promettons	tu promettrais	tu aurais promis
promettez	il promettrait	il aurait promis
	nous promettrions	nous aurions promis
	vous promettriez	vous auriez promis
	ils promettraient	ils auraient promis

SUBJUNCTIVE

PRESENT	IMPERFECT	PERFECT
je promette	je promisse	j'aie promis
tu promettes	tu promisses	tu aies promis
il promette	il promît	il ait promis
nous promettions	nous promissions	nous ayons promis
vous promettiez	vous promissiez	vous ayez promis
ils promettent	ils promissent	ils aient promis

INFINITIVE	PARTICIPLE
PRESENT	PRESENT
promettre	promettant
PAST	PAST
avoir promis	promis

PROMOUVOIR to promote

PRESENT	IMPERFECT	FUTURE

PAST HISTORIC	PERFECT	PLUPERFECT
	j'ai promu	j'avais promu
	tu as promu	tu avais promu
	il a promu	il avait promu
	nous avons promu	nous avions promu
	vous avez promu	vous aviez promu
	ils ont promu	ils avaient promu
PAST ANTERIOR	**FUTURE PERFECT**	
j'eus promu etc	j'aurai promu etc	

IMPERATIVE	CONDITIONAL PRESENT	CONDITIONAL PAST
		j'aurais promu
		tu aurais promu
		il aurait promu
		nous aurions promu
		vous auriez promu
		ils auraient promu

SUBJUNCTIVE

PRESENT	IMPERFECT	PERFECT
		j'aie promu
		tu aies promu
		il ait promu
		nous ayons promu
		vous ayez promu
		ils aient promu

INFINITIVE	PARTICIPLE
PRESENT	**PRESENT**
promouvoir	promouvant
PAST	**PAST**
avoir promu	promu

PRESENT	IMPERFECT	FUTURE
je protège	je protégeais	je protégerai
tu protèges	tu protégeais	tu protégeras
il protège	il protégeait	il protégera
nous protégeons	nous protégions	nous protégerons
vous protégez	vous protégiez	vous protégerez
ils protègent	ils protégeaient	ils protégeront
PAST HISTORIC	**PERFECT**	**PLUPERFECT**
je protégeai	j'ai protégé	j'avais protégé
tu protégeas	tu as protégé	tu avais protégé
il protégea	il a protégé	il avait protégé
nous protégeâmes	nous avons protégé	nous avions protégé
vous protégeâtes	vous avez protégé	vous aviez protégé
ils protégèrent	ils ont protégé	ils avaient protégé
PAST ANTERIOR	**FUTURE PERFECT**	
j'eus protégé etc	j'aurai protégé etc	

IMPERATIVE	CONDITIONAL PRESENT	CONDITIONAL PAST
	je protégerais	j'aurais protégé
protège	tu protégerais	tu aurais protégé
protégeons	il protégerait	il aurait protégé
protégez	nous protégerions	nous aurions protégé
	vous protégeriez	vous auriez protégé
	ils protégeraient	ils auraient protégé

SUBJUNCTIVE

PRESENT	IMPERFECT	PERFECT
je protège	je protégeasse	j'aie protégé
tu protèges	tu protégeasses	tu aies protégé
il protège	il protégeât	il ait protégé
nous protégions	nous protégeassions	nous ayons protégé
vous protégiez	vous protégeassiez	vous ayez protégé
ils protègent	ils protégeassent	ils aient protégé

INFINITIVE	PARTICIPLE
PRESENT	**PRESENT**
protéger	protégeant
PAST	**PAST**
avoir protégé	protégé

PRESENT	IMPERFECT	FUTURE
je pue	je puais	je puerai
tu pues	tu puais	tu pueras
il pue	il puait	il puera
nous puons	nous puions	nous puerons
vous puez	vous puiez	vous puerez
ils puent	ils puaient	ils pueront
PAST HISTORIC	**PERFECT**	**PLUPERFECT**
	j'ai pué	j'avais pué
	tu as pué	tu avais pué
	il a pué	il avait pué
	nous avons pué	nous avions pué
	vous avez pué	vous aviez pué
	ils ont pué	ils avaient pué
PAST ANTERIOR	**FUTURE PERFECT**	
j'eus pué etc	j'aurai pué etc	

IMPERATIVE	CONDITIONAL PRESENT	CONDITIONAL PAST
	je puerais	j'aurais pué
	tu puerais	tu aurais pué
	il puerait	il aurait pué
	nous puerions	nous aurions pué
	vous pueriez	vous auriez pué
	ils pueraient	ils auraient pué

SUBJUNCTIVE

PRESENT	IMPERFECT	PERFECT
je pue		j'aie pué
tu pues		tu aies pué
il pue		il ait pué
nous puions		nous ayons pué
vous puiez		vous ayez pué
ils puent		ils aient pué

INFINITIVE	PARTICIPLE
PRESENT	**PRESENT**
puer	puant
PAST	**PAST**
avoir pué	pué

PRESENT	IMPERFECT	FUTURE
je rapièce	je rapiéçais	je rapiécerai
tu rapièces	tu rapiéçais	tu rapiéceras
il rapièce	il rapiéçait	il rapiécera
nous rapiéçons	nous rapiécions	nous rapiécerons
vous rapiécez	vous rapiéciez	vous rapiécerez
ils rapiècent	ils rapiéçaient	ils rapiéceront
PAST HISTORIC	**PERFECT**	**PLUPERFECT**
je rapiéçai	j'ai rapiécé	j'avais rapiécé
tu rapiéças	tu as rapiécé	tu avais rapiécé
il rapiéça	il a rapiécé	il avait rapiécé
nous rapiéçâmes	nous avons rapiécé	nous avions rapiécé
vous rapiéçâtes	vous avez rapiécé	vous aviez rapiécé
ils rapiécèrent	ils ont rapiécé	ils avaient rapiécé
PAST ANTERIOR	**FUTURE PERFECT**	
j'eus rapiécé etc	j'aurai rapiécé etc	

IMPERATIVE	CONDITIONAL PRESENT	CONDITIONAL PAST
rapièce	je rapiécerais	j'aurais rapiécé
rapiéçons	tu rapiécerais	tu aurais rapiécé
rapiécez	il rapiécerait	il aurait rapiécé
	nous rapiécerions	nous aurions rapiécé
	vous rapiéceriez	vous auriez rapiécé
	ils rapiéceraient	ils auraient rapiécé

SUBJUNCTIVE

PRESENT	IMPERFECT	PERFECT
je rapièce	je rapiéçasse	j'aie rapiécé
tu rapièces	tu rapiéçasses	tu aies rapiécé
il rapièce	il rapiéçât	il ait rapiécé
nous rapiécions	nous rapiéçassions	nous ayons rapiécé
vous rapiéciez	vous rapiéçassiez	vous ayez rapiécé
ils rapiècent	ils rapiéçassent	ils aient rapiécé

INFINITIVE	PARTICIPLE
PRESENT	**PRESENT**
rapiécer	rapiéçant
PAST	**PAST**
avoir rapiécé	rapiécé

PRESENT	IMPERFECT	FUTURE
je reçois	je recevais	je recevrai
tu reçois	tu recevais	tu recevras
il reçoit	il recevait	il recevra
nous recevons	nous recevions	nous recevrons
vous recevez	vous receviez	vous recevrez
ils reçoivent	ils recevaient	ils recevront
PAST HISTORIC	**PERFECT**	**PLUPERFECT**
je reçus	j'ai reçu	j'avais reçu
tu reçus	tu as reçu	tu avais reçu
il reçut	il a reçu	il avait reçu
nous reçûmes	nous avons reçu	nous avions reçu
vous reçûtes	vous avez reçu	vous aviez reçu
ils reçurent	ils ont reçu	ils avaient reçu
PAST ANTERIOR	**FUTURE PERFECT**	
j'eus reçu etc	j'aurai reçu etc	

IMPERATIVE	CONDITIONAL PRESENT	CONDITIONAL PAST
reçois	je recevrais	j'aurais reçu
recevons	tu recevrais	tu aurais reçu
recevez	il recevrait	il aurait reçu
	nous recevrions	nous aurions reçu
	vous recevriez	vous auriez reçu
	ils recevraient	ils auraient reçu

SUBJUNCTIVE

PRESENT	IMPERFECT	PERFECT
je reçoive	je reçusse	j'aie reçu
tu reçoives	tu reçusses	tu aies reçu
il reçoive	il reçût	il ait reçu
nous recevions	nous reçussions	nous ayons reçu
vous receviez	vous reçussiez	vous ayez reçu
ils reçoivent	ils reçussent	ils aient reçu

INFINITIVE	PARTICIPLE
PRESENT	**PRESENT**
recevoir	recevant
PAST	**PAST**
avoir reçu	reçu

PRESENT	IMPERFECT	FUTURE
je réfrène	je réfrénais	je réfrénerai
tu réfrènes	tu réfrénais	tu réfréneras
il réfrène	il réfrénait	il réfrénera
nous réfrénons	nous réfrénions	nous réfrénerons
vous réfrénez	vous réfréniez	vous réfrénerez
ils réfrènent	ils réfrénaient	ils réfréneront
PAST HISTORIC	**PERFECT**	**PLUPERFECT**
je réfrénai	j'ai réfréné	j'avais réfréné
tu réfrénas	tu as réfréné	tu avais réfréné
il réfréna	il a réfréné	il avait réfréné
nous réfrénâmes	nous avons réfréné	nous avions réfréné
vous réfrénâtes	vous avez réfréné	vous aviez réfréné
ils réfrénèrent	ils ont réfréné	ils avaient réfréné
PAST ANTERIOR	**FUTURE PERFECT**	
j'eus réfréné etc	j'aurai réfréné etc	

IMPERATIVE	CONDITIONAL PRESENT	CONDITIONAL PAST
	je réfrénerais	j'aurais réfréné
réfrène	tu réfrénerais	tu aurais réfréné
réfrénons	il réfrénerait	il aurait réfréné
réfrénez	nous réfrénerions	nous aurions réfréné
	vous réfréneriez	vous auriez réfréné
	ils réfréneraient	ils auraient réfréné

SUBJUNCTIVE

PRESENT	IMPERFECT	PERFECT
je réfrène	je réfrénasse	j'aie réfréné
tu réfrènes	tu réfrénasses	tu aies réfréné
il réfrène	il réfrénât	il ait réfréné
nous réfrénions	nous réfrénassions	nous ayons réfréné
vous réfréniez	vous réfrénassiez	vous ayez réfréné
ils réfrènent	ils réfrénassent	ils aient réfréné

INFINITIVE	PARTICIPLE
PRESENT	**PRESENT**
réfréner	réfrénant
PAST	**PAST**
avoir réfréné	réfréné

PRESENT	IMPERFECT	FUTURE
je règle	je réglais	je réglerai
tu règles	tu réglais	tu régleras
il règle	il réglait	il réglera
nous réglons	nous réglions	nous réglerons
vous réglez	vous régliez	vous réglerez
ils règlent	ils réglaient	ils régleront
PAST HISTORIC	**PERFECT**	**PLUPERFECT**
je réglai	j'ai réglé	j'avais réglé
tu réglas	tu as réglé	tu avais réglé
il régla	il a réglé	il avait réglé
nous réglâmes	nous avons réglé	nous avions réglé
vous réglâtes	vous avez réglé	vous aviez réglé
ils réglèrent	ils ont réglé	ils avaient réglé
PAST ANTERIOR	**FUTURE PERFECT**	
j'eus réglé etc	j'aurai réglé etc	

IMPERATIVE	CONDITIONAL PRESENT	CONDITIONAL PAST
	je réglerais	j'aurais réglé
règle	tu réglerais	tu aurais réglé
réglons	il réglerait	il aurait réglé
réglez	nous réglerions	nous aurions réglé
	vous régleriez	vous auriez réglé
	ils régleraient	ils auraient réglé

SUBJUNCTIVE

PRESENT	IMPERFECT	PERFECT
je règle	je réglasse	j'aie réglé
tu règles	tu réglasses	tu aies réglé
il règle	il réglât	il ait réglé
nous réglions	nous réglassions	nous ayons réglé
vous régliez	vous réglassiez	vous ayez réglé
ils règlent	ils réglassent	ils aient réglé

INFINITIVE	PARTICIPLE
PRESENT	**PRESENT**
régler	réglant
PAST	**PAST**
avoir réglé	réglé

PRESENT	IMPERFECT	FUTURE
je règne	je régnais	je régnerai
tu règnes	tu régnais	tu régneras
il règne	il régnait	il régnera
nous régnons	nous régnions	nous régnerons
vous régnez	vous régniez	vous régnerez
ils règnent	ils régnaient	ils régneront
PAST HISTORIC	**PERFECT**	**PLUPERFECT**
je régnai	j'ai régné	j'avais régné
tu régnas	tu as régné	tu avais régné
il régna	il a régné	il avait régné
nous régnâmes	nous avons régné	nous avions régné
vous régnâtes	vous avez régné	vous aviez régné
ils régnèrent	ils ont régné	ils avaient régné
PAST ANTERIOR	**FUTURE PERFECT**	
j'eus régné etc	j'aurai régné etc	

IMPERATIVE	CONDITIONAL	
	PRESENT	**PAST**
règne	je régnerais	j'aurais régné
régnons	tu régnerais	tu aurais régné
régnez	il régnerait	il aurait régné
	nous régnerions	nous aurions régné
	vous régneriez	vous auriez régné
	ils régneraient	ils auraient régné

	SUBJUNCTIVE	
PRESENT	**IMPERFECT**	**PERFECT**
je règne	je régnasse	j'aie régné
tu règnes	tu régnasses	tu aies régné
il règne	il régnât	il ait régné
nous régnions	nous régnassions	nous ayons régné
vous régniez	vous régnassiez	vous ayez régné
ils règnent	ils régnassent	ils aient régné

INFINITIVE	PARTICIPLE
PRESENT	**PRESENT**
régner	régnant
PAST	**PAST**
avoir régné	régné

PRESENT	IMPERFECT	FUTURE
je renais	je renaissais	je renaîtrai
tu renais	tu renaissais	tu renaîtras
il renaît	il renaissait	il renaîtra
nous renaissons	nous renaissions	nous renaîtrons
vous renaissez	vous renaissiez	vous renaîtrez
ils renaissent	ils renaissaient	ils renaîtront

PAST HISTORIC	PERFECT	PLUPERFECT
je renaquis		
tu renaquis		
il renaquit		
nous renaquîmes		
vous renaquîtes		
ils renaquirent		

PAST ANTERIOR	FUTURE PERFECT

IMPERATIVE

renais
renaissons
renaissez

CONDITIONAL

PRESENT	PAST
je renaîtrais	
tu renaîtrais	
il renaîtrait	
nous renaîtrions	
vous renaîtriez	
ils renaîtraient	

SUBJUNCTIVE

PRESENT	IMPERFECT	PERFECT
je renaisse	je renaquisse	
tu renaisses	tu renaquisses	
il renaisse	il renaquît	
nous renaissions	nous renaquissions	
vous renaissiez	vous renaquissiez	
ils renaissent	ils renaquissent	

INFINITIVE	PARTICIPLE
PRESENT	PRESENT
renaître	renaissant
PAST	PAST

PRESENT	IMPERFECT	FUTURE
je rends	je rendais	je rendrai
tu rends	tu rendais	tu rendras
il rend	il rendait	il rendra
nous rendons	nous rendions	nous rendrons
vous rendez	vous rendiez	vous rendrez
ils rendent	ils rendaient	ils rendront
PAST HISTORIC	**PERFECT**	**PLUPERFECT**
je rendis	j'ai rendu	j'avais rendu
tu rendis	tu as rendu	tu avais rendu
il rendit	il a rendu	il avait rendu
nous rendîmes	nous avons rendu	nous avions rendu
vous rendîtes	vous avez rendu	vous aviez rendu
ils rendirent	ils ont rendu	ils avaient rendu
PAST ANTERIOR	**FUTURE PERFECT**	
j'eus rendu etc	j'aurai rendu etc	

IMPERATIVE	CONDITIONAL	
	PRESENT	**PAST**
rends	je rendrais	j'aurais rendu
rendons	tu rendrais	tu aurais rendu
rendez	il rendrait	il aurait rendu
	nous rendrions	nous aurions rendu
	vous rendriez	vous auriez rendu
	ils rendraient	ils auraient rendu

SUBJUNCTIVE

PRESENT	IMPERFECT	PERFECT
je rende	je rendisse	j'aie rendu
tu rendes	tu rendisses	tu aies rendu
il rende	il rendît	il ait rendu
nous rendions	nous rendissions	nous ayons rendu
vous rendiez	vous rendissiez	vous ayez rendu
ils rendent	ils rendissent	ils aient rendu

INFINITIVE	PARTICIPLE
PRESENT	**PRESENT**
rendre	rendant
PAST	**PAST**
avoir rendu	rendu

RENTRER to go home, to go in

PRESENT	IMPERFECT	FUTURE
je rentre	je rentrais	je rentrerai
tu rentres	tu rentrais	tu rentreras
il rentre	il rentrait	il rentrera
nous rentrons	nous rentrions	nous rentrerons
vous rentrez	vous rentriez	vous rentrerez
ils rentrent	ils rentraient	ils rentreront
PAST HISTORIC	**PERFECT**	**PLUPERFECT**
je rentrai	je suis rentré	j'étais rentré
tu rentras	tu es rentré	tu étais rentré
il rentra	il est rentré	il était rentré
nous rentrâmes	nous sommes rentrés	nous étions rentrés
vous rentrâtes	vous êtes rentré(s)	vous étiez rentré(s)
ils rentrèrent	ils sont rentrés	ils étaient rentrés
PAST ANTERIOR	**FUTURE PERFECT**	
je fus rentré etc	je serai rentré etc	

IMPERATIVE	CONDITIONAL PRESENT	CONDITIONAL PAST
	je rentrerais	je serais rentré
rentre	tu rentrerais	tu serais rentré
rentrons	il rentrerait	il serait rentré
rentrez	nous rentrerions	nous serions rentrés
	vous rentreriez	vous seriez rentré(s)
	ils rentreraient	ils seraient rentrés

SUBJUNCTIVE

PRESENT	IMPERFECT	PERFECT
je rentre	je rentrasse	je sois rentré
tu rentres	tu rentrasses	tu sois rentré
il rentre	il rentrât	il soit rentré
nous rentrions	nous rentrassions	nous soyons rentrés
vous rentriez	vous rentrassiez	vous soyez rentré(s)
ils rentrent	ils rentrassent	ils soient rentrés

INFINITIVE	PARTICIPLE	NOTE
PRESENT	**PRESENT**	**rentrer** takes the auxiliary 'avoir' when transitive
rentrer	rentrant	
PAST	**PAST**	
être rentré	rentré	

PRESENT	IMPERFECT	FUTURE
je répands	je répandais	je répandrai
tu répands	tu répandais	tu répandras
il répand	il répandait	il répandra
nous répandons	nous répandions	nous répandrons
vous répandez	vous répandiez	vous répandrez
ils répandent	ils répandaient	ils répandront
PAST HISTORIC	**PERFECT**	**PLUPERFECT**
je répandis	j'ai répandu	j'avais répandu
tu répandis	tu as répandu	tu avais répandu
il répandit	il a répandu	il avait répandu
nous répandîmes	nous avons répandu	nous avions répandu
vous répandîtes	vous avez répandu	vous aviez répandu
ils répandirent	ils ont répandu	ils avaient répandu
PAST ANTERIOR	**FUTURE PERFECT**	
j'eus répandu etc	j'aurai répandu etc	

IMPERATIVE	CONDITIONAL PRESENT	CONDITIONAL PAST
	je répandrais	j'aurais répandu
répands	tu répandrais	tu aurais répandu
répandons	il répandrait	il aurait répandu
répandez	nous répandrions	nous aurions répandu
	vous répandriez	vous auriez répandu
	ils répandraient	ils auraient répandu

SUBJUNCTIVE

PRESENT	IMPERFECT	PERFECT
je répande	je répandisse	j'aie répandu
tu répandes	tu répandisses	tu aies répandu
il répande	il répandît	il ait répandu
nous répandions	nous répandissions	nous ayons répandu
vous répandiez	vous répandissiez	vous ayez répandu
ils répandent	ils répandissent	ils aient répandu

INFINITIVE	PARTICIPLE
PRESENT	**PRESENT**
répandre	répandant
PAST	**PAST**
avoir répandu	répandu

PRESENT
je réponds
tu réponds
il répond
nous répondons
vous répondez
ils répondent

IMPERFECT
je répondais
tu répondais
il répondait
nous répondions
vous répondiez
ils répondaient

FUTURE
je répondrai
tu répondras
il répondra
nous répondrons
vous répondrez
ils répondront

PAST HISTORIC
je répondis
tu répondis
il répondit
nous répondîmes
vous répondîtes
ils répondirent

PERFECT
j'ai répondu
tu as répondu
il a répondu
nous avons répondu
vous avez répondu
ils ont répondu

PLUPERFECT
j'avais répondu
tu avais répondu
il avait répondu
nous avions répondu
vous aviez répondu
ils avaient répondu

PAST ANTERIOR
j'eus répondu etc

FUTURE PERFECT
j'aurai répondu etc

IMPERATIVE

réponds
répondons
répondez

CONDITIONAL

PRESENT
je répondrais
tu répondrais
il répondrait
nous répondrions
vous répondriez
ils répondraient

PAST
j'aurais répondu
tu aurais répondu
il aurait répondu
nous aurions répondu
vous auriez répondu
ils auraient répondu

SUBJUNCTIVE

PRESENT
je réponde
tu répondes
il réponde
nous répondions
vous répondiez
ils répondent

IMPERFECT
je répondisse
tu répondisses
il répondît
nous répondissions
vous répondissiez
ils répondissent

PERFECT
j'aie répondu
tu aies répondu
il ait répondu
nous ayons répondu
vous ayez répondu
ils aient répondu

INFINITIVE

PRESENT
répondre

PAST
avoir répondu

PARTICIPLE

PRESENT
répondant

PAST
répondu

PRESENT	IMPERFECT	FUTURE
je résous	je résolvais	je résoudrai
tu résous	tu résolvais	tu résoudras
il résout	il résolvait	il résoudra
nous résolvons	nous résolvions	nous résoudrons
vous résolvez	vous résolviez	vous résoudrez
ils résolvent	ils résolvaient	ils résoudront
PAST HISTORIC	**PERFECT**	**PLUPERFECT**
je résolus	j'ai résolu	j'avais résolu
tu résolus	tu as résolu	tu avais résolu
il résolut	il a résolu	il avait résolu
nous résolûmes	nous avons résolu	nous avions résolu
vous résolûtes	vous avez résolu	vous aviez résolu
ils résolurent	ils ont résolu	ils avaient résolu
PAST ANTERIOR	**FUTURE PERFECT**	
j'eus résolu etc	j'aurai résolu etc	

IMPERATIVE	CONDITIONAL PRESENT	CONDITIONAL PAST
	je résoudrais	j'aurais résolu
résous	tu résoudrais	tu aurais résolu
résolvons	il résoudrait	il aurait résolu
résolvez	nous résoudrions	nous aurions résolu
	vous résoudriez	vous auriez résolu
	ils résoudraient	ils auraient résolu

SUBJUNCTIVE

PRESENT	IMPERFECT	PERFECT
je résolve	je résolusse	j'aie résolu
tu résolves	tu résolusses	tu aies résolu
il résolve	il résolût	il ait résolu
nous résolvions	nous résolussions	nous ayons résolu
vous résolviez	vous résolussiez	vous ayez résolu
ils résolvent	ils résolussent	ils aient résolu

INFINITIVE	PARTICIPLE
PRESENT	**PRESENT**
résoudre	résolvant
PAST	**PAST**
avoir résolu	résolu

RESTER to stay 176

PRESENT	IMPERFECT	FUTURE
je reste	je restais	je resterai
tu restes	tu restais	tu resteras
il reste	il restait	il restera
nous restons	nous restions	nous resterons
vous restez	vous restiez	vous resterez
ils restent	ils restaient	ils resteront

PAST HISTORIC	PERFECT	PLUPERFECT
je restai	je suis resté	j'étais resté
tu restas	tu es resté	tu étais resté
il resta	il est resté	il était resté
nous restâmes	nous sommes restés	nous étions restés
vous restâtes	vous êtes resté(s)	vous étiez resté(s)
ils restèrent	ils sont restés	ils étaient restés

PAST ANTERIOR	FUTURE PERFECT
je fus resté etc	je serai resté etc

IMPERATIVE	CONDITIONAL	
	PRESENT	PAST
	je resterais	je serais resté
reste	tu resterais	tu serais resté
restons	il resterait	il serait resté
restez	nous resterions	nous serions restés
	vous resteriez	vous seriez resté(s)
	ils resteraient	ils seraient restés

	SUBJUNCTIVE	
PRESENT	IMPERFECT	PERFECT
je reste	je restasse	je sois resté
tu restes	tu restasses	tu sois resté
il reste	il restât	il soit resté
nous restions	nous restassions	nous soyons restés
vous restiez	vous restassiez	vous soyez resté(s)
ils restent	ils restassent	ils soient restés

INFINITIVE	PARTICIPLE
PRESENT	PRESENT
rester	restant
PAST	PAST
être resté	resté

RETOURNER to return

PRESENT	IMPERFECT	FUTURE
je retourne	je retournais	je retournerai
tu retournes	tu retournais	tu retourneras
il retourne	il retournait	il retournera
nous retournons	nous retournions	nous retournerons
vous retournez	vous retourniez	vous retournerez
ils retournent	ils retournaient	ils retourneront
PAST HISTORIC	**PERFECT**	**PLUPERFECT**
je retournai	je suis retourné	j'étais retourné
tu retournas	tu es retourné	tu étais retourné
il retourna	il est retourné	il était retourné
nous retournâmes	nous sommes retournés	nous étions retournés
vous retournâtes	vous êtes retourné(s)	vous étiez retourné(s)
ils retournèrent	ils sont retournés	ils étaient retournés
PAST ANTERIOR	**FUTURE PERFECT**	
je fus retourné etc	je serai retourné etc	

IMPERATIVE	CONDITIONAL PRESENT	CONDITIONAL PAST
	je retournerais	je serais retourné
retourne	tu retournerais	tu serais retourné
retournons	il retournerait	il serait retourné
retournez	nous retournerions	nous serions retournés
	vous retourneriez	vous seriez retourné(s)
	ils retourneraient	ils seraient retournés

SUBJUNCTIVE

PRESENT	IMPERFECT	PERFECT
je retourne	je retournasse	je sois retourné
tu retournes	tu retournasses	tu sois retourné
il retourne	il retournât	il soit retourné
nous retournions	nous retournassions	nous soyons retournés
vous retourniez	vous retournassiez	vous soyez retourné(s)
ils retournent	ils retournassent	ils soient retournés

INFINITIVE	PARTICIPLE	NOTE
PRESENT	**PRESENT**	**retourner** takes the auxiliary 'avoir' when transitive
retourner	retournant	
PAST	**PAST**	
être retourné	retourné	

PRESENT	IMPERFECT	FUTURE
je révèle	je révélais	je révélerai
tu révèles	tu révélais	tu révéleras
il révèle	il révélait	il révélera
nous révélons	nous révélions	nous révélerons
vous révélez	vous révéliez	vous révélerez
ils révèlent	ils révélaient	ils révéleront
PAST HISTORIC	**PERFECT**	**PLUPERFECT**
je révélai	j'ai révélé	j'avais révélé
tu révélas	tu as révélé	tu avais révélé
il révéla	il a révélé	il avait révélé
nous révélâmes	nous avons révélé	nous avions révélé
vous révélâtes	vous avez révélé	vous aviez révélé
ils révélèrent	ils ont révélé	ils avaient révélé
PAST ANTERIOR	**FUTURE PERFECT**	
j'eus révélé etc	j'aurai révélé etc	

IMPERATIVE	CONDITIONAL PRESENT	CONDITIONAL PAST
	je révélerais	j'aurais révélé
révèle	tu révélerais	tu aurais révélé
révélons	il révélerait	il aurait révélé
révélez	nous révélerions	nous aurions révélé
	vous révéleriez	vous auriez révélé
	ils révéleraient	ils auraient révélé

SUBJUNCTIVE

PRESENT	IMPERFECT	PERFECT
je révèle	je révélasse	j'aie révélé
tu révèles	tu révélasses	tu aies révélé
il révèle	il révélât	il ait révélé
nous révélions	nous révélassions	nous ayons révélé
vous révéliez	vous révélassiez	vous ayez révélé
ils révèlent	ils révélassent	ils aient révélé

INFINITIVE	PARTICIPLE
PRESENT	**PRESENT**
révéler	révélant
PAST	**PAST**
avoir révélé	révélé

REVENIR to come back

PRESENT	IMPERFECT	FUTURE
je reviens	je revenais	je reviendrai
tu reviens	tu revenais	tu reviendras
il revient	il revenait	il reviendra
nous revenons	nous revenions	nous reviendrons
vous revenez	vous reveniez	vous reviendrez
ils reviennent	ils revenaient	ils reviendront
PAST HISTORIC	**PERFECT**	**PLUPERFECT**
je revins	je suis revenu	j'étais revenu
tu revins	tu es revenu	tu étais revenu
il revint	il est revenu	il était revenu
nous revînmes	nous sommes revenus	nous étions revenus
vous revîntes	vous êtes revenu(s)	vous étiez revenu(s)
ils revinrent	ils sont revenus	ils étaient revenus
PAST ANTERIOR	**FUTURE PERFECT**	
je fus revenu etc	je serai revenu etc	

IMPERATIVE	CONDITIONAL	
	PRESENT	**PAST**
reviens	je reviendrais	je serais revenu
revenons	tu reviendrais	tu serais revenu
revenez	il reviendrait	il serait revenu
	nous reviendrions	nous serions revenus
	vous reviendriez	vous seriez revenu(s)
	ils reviendraient	ils seraient revenus

	SUBJUNCTIVE	
PRESENT	**IMPERFECT**	**PERFECT**
je revienne	je revinsse	je sois revenu
tu reviennes	tu revinsses	tu sois revenu
il revienne	il revînt	il soit revenu
nous revenions	nous revinssions	nous soyons revenus
vous reveniez	vous revinssiez	vous soyez revenu(s)
ils reviennent	ils revinssent	ils soient revenus

INFINITIVE	PARTICIPLE
PRESENT	**PRESENT**
revenir	revenant
PAST	**PAST**
être revenu	revenu

PRESENT	IMPERFECT	FUTURE
je ris	je riais	je rirai
tu ris	tu riais	tu riras
il rit	il riait	il rira
nous rions	nous riions	nous rirons
vous riez	vous riiez	vous rirez
ils rient	ils riaient	ils riront
PAST HISTORIC	**PERFECT**	**PLUPERFECT**
je ris	j'ai ri	j'avais ri
tu ris	tu as ri	tu avais ri
il rit	il a ri	il avait ri
nous rîmes	nous avons ri	nous avions ri
vous rîtes	vous avez ri	vous aviez ri
ils rirent	ils ont ri	ils avaient ri
PAST ANTERIOR	**FUTURE PERFECT**	
j'eus ri etc	j'aurai ri etc	

IMPERATIVE	CONDITIONAL	
	PRESENT	PAST
ris	je rirais	j'aurais ri
rions	tu rirais	tu aurais ri
riez	il rirait	il aurait ri
	nous ririons	nous aurions ri
	vous ririez	vous auriez ri
	ils riraient	ils auraient ri

	SUBJUNCTIVE	
PRESENT	IMPERFECT	PERFECT
je rie	je risse	j'aie ri
tu ries	tu risses	tu aies ri
il rie	il rît	il ait ri
nous riions	nous rissions	nous ayons ri
vous riiez	vous rissiez	vous ayez ri
ils rient	ils rissent	ils aient ri

INFINITIVE	PARTICIPLE
PRESENT	PRESENT
rire	riant
PAST	PAST
avoir ri	ri

PRESENT	IMPERFECT	FUTURE
je romps	je rompais	je romprai
tu romps	tu rompais	tu rompras
il rompt	il rompait	il rompra
nous rompons	nous rompions	nous romprons
vous rompez	vous rompiez	vous romprez
ils rompent	ils rompaient	ils rompront
PAST HISTORIC	**PERFECT**	**PLUPERFECT**
je rompis	j'ai rompu	j'avais rompu
tu rompis	tu as rompu	tu avais rompu
il rompit	il a rompu	il avait rompu
nous rompîmes	nous avons rompu	nous avions rompu
vous rompîtes	vous avez rompu	vous aviez rompu
ils rompirent	ils ont rompu	ils avaient rompu
PAST ANTERIOR	**FUTURE PERFECT**	
j'eus rompu etc	j'aurai rompu etc	

IMPERATIVE	CONDITIONAL PRESENT	CONDITIONAL PAST
	je romprais	j'aurais rompu
romps	tu romprais	tu aurais rompu
rompons	il romprait	il aurait rompu
rompez	nous romprions	nous aurions rompu
	vous rompriez	vous auriez rompu
	ils rompraient	ils auraient rompu

SUBJUNCTIVE

PRESENT	IMPERFECT	PERFECT
je rompe	je rompisse	j'aie rompu
tu rompes	tu rompisses	tu aies rompu
il rompe	il rompît	il ait rompu
nous rompions	nous rompissions	nous ayons rompu
vous rompiez	vous rompissiez	vous ayez rompu
ils rompent	ils rompissent	ils aient rompu

INFINITIVE	PARTICIPLE
PRESENT	**PRESENT**
rompre	rompant
PAST	**PAST**
avoir rompu	rompu

PRESENT	IMPERFECT	FUTURE
il saille	il saillait	il saillera
ils saillent	ils saillaient	ils sailleront

PAST HISTORIC	PERFECT	PLUPERFECT
il saillit	il a sailli	il avait sailli
ils saillirent	ils ont sailli	ils avaient sailli

PAST ANTERIOR	FUTURE PERFECT
il eut sailli etc	il aura sailli etc

IMPERATIVE

CONDITIONAL

PRESENT	PAST
il saillerait	il aurait sailli
ils sailleraient	ils auraient sailli

SUBJUNCTIVE

PRESENT	IMPERFECT	PERFECT
il saille	il saillît	il ait sailli
ils saillent	ils saillissent	ils aient sailli

INFINITIVE	PARTICIPLE
PRESENT	**PRESENT**
saillir	saillant
PAST	**PAST**
avoir sailli	sailli

PRESENT	IMPERFECT	FUTURE
je sais	je savais	je saurai
tu sais	tu savais	tu sauras
il sait	il savait	il saura
nous savons	nous savions	nous saurons
vous savez	vous saviez	vous saurez
ils savent	ils savaient	ils sauront
PAST HISTORIC	**PERFECT**	**PLUPERFECT**
je sus	j'ai su	j'avais su
tu sus	tu as su	tu avais su
il sut	il a su	il avait su
nous sûmes	nous avons su	nous avions su
vous sûtes	vous avez su	vous aviez su
ils surent	ils ont su	ils avaient su
PAST ANTERIOR	**FUTURE PERFECT**	
j'eus su etc	j'aurai su etc	

IMPERATIVE	CONDITIONAL PRESENT	CONDITIONAL PAST
sache	je saurais	j'aurais su
sachons	tu saurais	tu aurais su
sachez	il saurait	il aurait su
	nous saurions	nous aurions su
	vous sauriez	vous auriez su
	ils sauraient	ils auraient su

SUBJUNCTIVE

PRESENT	IMPERFECT	PERFECT
je sache	je susse	j'aie su
tu saches	tu susses	tu aies su
il sache	il sût	il ait su
nous sachions	nous sussions	nous ayons su
vous sachiez	vous sussiez	vous ayez su
ils sachent	ils sussent	ils aient su

INFINITIVE	PARTICIPLE
PRESENT	**PRESENT**
savoir	sachant
PAST	**PAST**
avoir su	su

PRESENT	IMPERFECT	FUTURE
je sèche	je séchais	je sécherai
tu sèches	tu séchais	tu sécheras
il sèche	il séchait	il séchera
nous séchons	nous séchions	nous sécherons
vous séchez	vous séchiez	vous sécherez
ils sèchent	ils séchaient	ils sécheront
PAST HISTORIC	**PERFECT**	**PLUPERFECT**
je séchai	j'ai séché	j'avais séché
tu séchas	tu as séché	tu avais séché
il sécha	il a séché	il avait séché
nous séchâmes	nous avons séché	nous avions séché
vous séchâtes	vous avez séché	vous aviez séché
ils séchèrent	ils ont séché	ils avaient séché
PAST ANTERIOR	**FUTURE PERFECT**	
j'eus séché etc	j'aurai séché etc	

IMPERATIVE	CONDITIONAL PRESENT	CONDITIONAL PAST
sèche	je sécherais	j'aurais séché
séchons	tu sécherais	tu aurais séché
séchez	il sécherait	il aurait séché
	nous sécherions	nous aurions séché
	vous sécheriez	vous auriez séché
	ils sécheraient	ils auraient séché

SUBJUNCTIVE

PRESENT	IMPERFECT	PERFECT
je sèche	je séchasse	j'aie séché
tu sèches	tu séchasses	tu aies séché
il sèche	il séchât	il ait séché
nous séchions	nous séchassions	nous ayons séché
vous séchiez	vous séchassiez	vous ayez séché
ils sèchent	ils séchassent	ils aient séché

INFINITIVE	PARTICIPLE
PRESENT	**PRESENT**
sécher	séchant
PAST	**PAST**
avoir séché	séché

PRESENT	IMPERFECT	FUTURE
je sème	je semais	je sèmerai
tu sèmes	tu semais	tu sèmeras
il sème	il semait	il sèmera
nous semons	nous semions	nous sèmerons
vous semez	vous semiez	vous sèmerez
ils sèment	ils semaient	ils sèmeront
PAST HISTORIC	**PERFECT**	**PLUPERFECT**
je semai	j'ai semé	j'avais semé
tu semas	tu as semé	tu avais semé
il sema	il a semé	il avait semé
nous semâmes	nous avons semé	nous avions semé
vous semâtes	vous avez semé	vous aviez semé
ils semèrent	ils ont semé	ils avaient semé
PAST ANTERIOR	**FUTURE PERFECT**	
j'eus semé etc	j'aurai semé etc	

IMPERATIVE	CONDITIONAL PRESENT	CONDITIONAL PAST
sème	je sèmerais	j'aurais semé
semons	tu sèmerais	tu aurais semé
semez	il sèmerait	il aurait semé
	nous sèmerions	nous aurions semé
	vous sèmeriez	vous auriez semé
	ils sèmeraient	ils auraient semé

SUBJUNCTIVE

PRESENT	IMPERFECT	PERFECT
je sème	je semasse	j'aie semé
tu sèmes	tu semasses	tu aies semé
il sème	il semât	il ait semé
nous semions	nous semassions	nous ayons semé
vous semiez	vous semassiez	vous ayez semé
ils sèment	ils semassent	ils aient semé

INFINITIVE	PARTICIPLE
PRESENT	**PRESENT**
semer	semant
PAST	**PAST**
avoir semé	semé

PRESENT	IMPERFECT	FUTURE
je sens	je sentais	je sentirai
tu sens	tu sentais	tu sentiras
il sent	il sentait	il sentira
nous sentons	nous sentions	nous sentirons
vous sentez	vous sentiez	vous sentirez
ils sentent	ils sentaient	ils sentiront
PAST HISTORIC	**PERFECT**	**PLUPERFECT**
je sentis	j'ai senti	j'avais senti
tu sentis	tu as senti	tu avais senti
il sentit	il a senti	il avait senti
nous sentîmes	nous avons senti	nous avions senti
vous sentîtes	vous avez senti	vous aviez senti
ils sentirent	ils ont senti	ils avaient senti
PAST ANTERIOR	**FUTURE PERFECT**	
j'eus senti etc	j'aurai senti etc	

IMPERATIVE	CONDITIONAL	
	PRESENT	**PAST**
sens	je sentirais	j'aurais senti
sentons	tu sentirais	tu aurais senti
sentez	il sentirait	il aurait senti
	nous sentirions	nous aurions senti
	vous sentiriez	vous auriez senti
	ils sentiraient	ils auraient senti

	SUBJUNCTIVE	
PRESENT	**IMPERFECT**	**PERFECT**
je sente	je sentisse	j'aie senti
tu sentes	tu sentisses	tu aies senti
il sente	il sentît	il ait senti
nous sentions	nous sentissions	nous ayons senti
vous sentiez	vous sentissiez	vous ayez senti
ils sentent	ils sentissent	ils aient senti

INFINITIVE	PARTICIPLE
PRESENT	**PRESENT**
sentir	sentant
PAST	**PAST**
avoir senti	senti

PRESENT	IMPERFECT	FUTURE
il sied ils siéent	il seyait ils seyaient	il siéra ils siéront

PAST HISTORIC	PERFECT	PLUPERFECT

PAST ANTERIOR	FUTURE PERFECT

IMPERATIVE

CONDITIONAL

PRESENT	PAST
il siérait ils siéraient	

SUBJUNCTIVE

PRESENT	IMPERFECT	PERFECT
il siée ils siéent		

INFINITIVE	PARTICIPLE
PRESENT	**PRESENT**
seoir	seyant
PAST	**PAST**

PRESENT	IMPERFECT	FUTURE
je serre	je serrais	je serrerai
tu serres	tu serrais	tu serreras
il serre	il serrait	il serrera
nous serrons	nous serrions	nous serrerons
vous serrez	vous serriez	vous serrerez
ils serrent	ils serraient	ils serreront
PAST HISTORIC	**PERFECT**	**PLUPERFECT**
je serrai	j'ai serré	j'avais serré
tu serras	tu as serré	tu avais serré
il serra	il a serré	il avait serré
nous serrâmes	nous avons serré	nous avions serré
vous serrâtes	vous avez serré	vous aviez serré
ils serrèrent	ils ont serré	ils avaient serré
PAST ANTERIOR	**FUTURE PERFECT**	
j'eus serré etc	j'aurai serré etc	

IMPERATIVE	CONDITIONAL	
	PRESENT	**PAST**
serre	je serrerais	j'aurais serré
serrons	tu serrerais	tu aurais serré
serrez	il serrerait	il aurait serré
	nous serrerions	nous aurions serré
	vous serreriez	vous auriez serré
	ils serreraient	ils auraient serré

	SUBJUNCTIVE	
PRESENT	**IMPERFECT**	**PERFECT**
je serre	je serrasse	j'aie serré
tu serres	tu serrasses	tu aies serré
il serre	il serrât	il ait serré
nous serrions	nous serrassions	nous ayons serré
vous serriez	vous serrassiez	vous ayez serré
ils serrent	ils serrassent	ils aient serré

INFINITIVE	PARTICIPLE
PRESENT	**PRESENT**
serrer	serrant
PAST	**PAST**
avoir serré	serré

PRESENT	IMPERFECT	FUTURE
je sers	je servais	je servirai
tu sers	tu servais	tu serviras
il sert	il servait	il servira
nous servons	nous servions	nous servirons
vous servez	vous serviez	vous servirez
ils servent	ils servaient	ils serviront
PAST HISTORIC	**PERFECT**	**PLUPERFECT**
je servis	j'ai servi	j'avais servi
tu servis	tu as servi	tu avais servi
il servit	il a servi	il avait servi
nous servîmes	nous avons servi	nous avions servi
vous servîtes	vous avez servi	vous aviez servi
ils servirent	ils ont servi	ils avaient servi
PAST ANTERIOR	**FUTURE PERFECT**	
j'eus servi etc	j'aurai servi etc	

IMPERATIVE	CONDITIONAL PRESENT	CONDITIONAL PAST
	je servirais	j'aurais servi
sers	tu servirais	tu aurais servi
servons	il servirait	il aurait servi
servez	nous servirions	nous aurions servi
	vous serviriez	vous auriez servi
	ils serviraient	ils auraient servi

SUBJUNCTIVE

PRESENT	IMPERFECT	PERFECT
je serve	je servisse	j'aie servi
tu serves	tu servisses	tu aies servi
il serve	il servît	il ait servi
nous servions	nous servissions	nous ayons servi
vous serviez	vous servissiez	vous ayez servi
ils servent	ils servissent	ils aient servi

INFINITIVE	PARTICIPLE
PRESENT	**PRESENT**
servir	servant
PAST	**PAST**
avoir servi	servi

PRESENT	IMPERFECT	FUTURE
je sèvre	je sevrais	je sèvrerai
tu sèvres	tu sevrais	tu sèvreras
il sèvre	il sevrait	il sèvrera
nous sevrons	nous sevrions	nous sèvrerons
vous sevrez	vous sevriez	vous sèvrerez
ils sèvrent	ils sevraient	ils sèvreront
PAST HISTORIC	**PERFECT**	**PLUPERFECT**
je sevrai	j'ai sevré	j'avais sevré
tu sevras	tu as sevré	tu avais sevré
il sevra	il a sevré	il avait sevré
nous sevrâmes	nous avons sevré	nous avions sevré
vous sevrâtes	vous avez sevré	vous aviez sevré
ils sevrèrent	ils ont sevré	ils avaient sevré
PAST ANTERIOR	**FUTURE PERFECT**	
j'eus sevré etc	j'aurai sevré etc	

IMPERATIVE	CONDITIONAL PRESENT	CONDITIONAL PAST
	je sèvrerais	j'aurais sevré
sèvre	tu sèvrerais	tu aurais sevré
sevrons	il sèvrerait	il aurait sevré
sevrez	nous sèvrerions	nous aurions sevré
	vous sèvreriez	vous auriez sevré
	ils sèvreraient	ils auraient sevré

SUBJUNCTIVE

PRESENT	IMPERFECT	PERFECT
je sèvre	je sevrasse	j'aie sevré
tu sèvres	tu sevrasses	tu aies sevré
il sèvre	il sevrât	il ait sevré
nous sevrions	nous sevrassions	nous ayons sevré
vous sevriez	vous sevrassiez	vous ayez sevré
ils sèvrent	ils sevrassent	ils aient sevré

INFINITIVE	PARTICIPLE
PRESENT	**PRESENT**
sevrer	sevrant
PAST	**PAST**
avoir sevré	sevré

PRESENT	IMPERFECT	FUTURE
je sors	je sortais	je sortirai
tu sors	tu sortais	tu sortiras
il sort	il sortait	il sortira
nous sortons	nous sortions	nous sortirons
vous sortez	vous sortiez	vous sortirez
ils sortent	ils sortaient	ils sortiront
PAST HISTORIC	**PERFECT**	**PLUPERFECT**
je sortis	je suis sorti	j'étais sorti
tu sortis	tu es sorti	tu étais sorti
il sortit	il est sorti	il était sorti
nous sortîmes	nous sommes sortis	nous étions sortis
vous sortîtes	vous êtes sorti(s)	vous étiez sorti(s)
ils sortirent	ils sont sortis	ils étaient sortis
PAST ANTERIOR	**FUTURE PERFECT**	
je fus sorti etc	je serai sorti etc	

IMPERATIVE	CONDITIONAL	
	PRESENT	**PAST**
sors	je sortirais	je serais sorti
sortons	tu sortirais	tu serais sorti
sortez	il sortirait	il serait sorti
	nous sortirions	nous serions sortis
	vous sortiriez	vous seriez sorti(s)
	ils sortiraient	ils seraient sortis

	SUBJUNCTIVE	
PRESENT	**IMPERFECT**	**PERFECT**
je sorte	je sortisse	je sois sorti
tu sortes	tu sortisses	tu sois sorti
il sorte	il sortît	il soit sorti
nous sortions	nous sortissions	nous soyons sortis
vous sortiez	vous sortissiez	vous soyez sorti(s)
ils sortent	ils sortissent	ils soient sortis

INFINITIVE	PARTICIPLE
PRESENT	**PRESENT**
sortir	sortant
PAST	**PAST**
être sorti	sorti

SE SOUVENIR to remember

PRESENT	IMPERFECT	FUTURE
je me souviens	je me souvenais	je me souviendrai
tu te souviens	tu te souvenais	tu te souviendras
il se souvient	il se souvenait	il se souviendra
nous nous souvenons	nous nous souvenions	nous nous souviendrons
vous vous souvenez	vous vous souveniez	vous vous souviendrez
ils se souviennent	ils se souvenaient	ils se souviendront
PAST HISTORIC	**PERFECT**	**PLUPERFECT**
je me souvins	je me suis souvenu	je m'étais souvenu
tu te souvins	tu t'es souvenu	tu t'étais souvenu
il se souvint	il s'est souvenu	il s'était souvenu
nous nous souvînmes	nous ns. sommes souvenus	nous ns. étions souvenus
vous vous souvîntes	vous vs. êtes souvenu(s)	vous vs. étiez souvenu(s)
ils se souvinrent	ils se sont souvenus	ils s'étaient souvenus
PAST ANTERIOR	**FUTURE PERFECT**	
je me fus souvenu etc	je me serai souvenu etc	

IMPERATIVE

souviens-toi
souvenons-nous
souvenez-vous

CONDITIONAL

PRESENT	PAST
je me souviendrais	je me serais souvenu
tu te souviendrais	tu te serais souvenu
il se souviendrait	il se serait souvenu
nous ns. souviendrions	nous ns. serions souvenus
vous vous souviendriez	vous vs. seriez souvenu(s)
ils se souviendraient	ils se seraient souvenus

SUBJUNCTIVE

PRESENT	IMPERFECT	PERFECT
je me souvienne	je me souvinsse	je me sois souvenu
tu te souviennes	tu te souvinsses	tu te sois souvenu
il se souvienne	il se souvînt	il se soit souvenu
nous nous souvenions	nous nous souvinssions	nous ns. soyons souvenus
vous vous souveniez	vous vous souvinssiez	vous vs. soyez souvenu(s)
ils se souviennent	ils se souvinssent	ils se soient souvenus

INFINITIVE	PARTICIPLE
PRESENT	**PRESENT**
se souvenir	se souvenant
PAST	**PAST**
s'être souvenu	souvenu

PRESENT	IMPERFECT	FUTURE
il stupéfait		

PAST HISTORIC	PERFECT	PLUPERFECT
	j'ai stupéfait	j'avais stupéfait
	tu as stupéfait	tu avais stupéfait
	il a stupéfait	il avait stupéfait
	nous avons stupéfait	nous avions stupéfait
	vous avez stupéfait	vous aviez stupéfait
	ils ont stupéfait	ils avaient stupéfait

PAST ANTERIOR	FUTURE PERFECT
j'eus stupéfait etc	j'aurai stupéfait etc

IMPERATIVE	CONDITIONAL PRESENT	CONDITIONAL PAST
		j'aurais stupéfait
		tu aurais stupéfait
		il aurait stupéfait
		nous aurions stupéfait
		vous auriez stupéfait
		ils auraient stupéfait

SUBJUNCTIVE

PRESENT	IMPERFECT	PERFECT
		j'aie stupéfait
		tu aies stupéfait
		il ait stupéfait
		nous ayons stupéfait
		vous ayez stupéfait
		ils aient stupéfait

INFINITIVE	PARTICIPLE
PRESENT	PRESENT
stupéfaire	
PAST	PAST
avoir stupéfait	stupéfait

PRESENT	IMPERFECT	FUTURE
je suffis	je suffisais	je suffirai
tu suffis	tu suffisais	tu suffiras
il suffit	il suffisait	il suffira
nous suffisons	nous suffisions	nous suffirons
vous suffisez	vous suffisiez	vous suffirez
ils suffisent	ils suffisaient	ils suffiront
PAST HISTORIC	**PERFECT**	**PLUPERFECT**
je suffis	j'ai suffi	j'avais suffi
tu suffis	tu as suffi	tu avais suffi
il suffit	il a suffi	il avait suffi
nous suffîmes	nous avons suffi	nous avions suffi
vous suffîtes	vous avez suffi	vous aviez suffi
ils suffirent	ils ont suffi	ils avaient suffi
PAST ANTERIOR	**FUTURE PERFECT**	
j'eus suffi etc	j'aurai suffi etc	

IMPERATIVE	CONDITIONAL	
	PRESENT	**PAST**
suffis	je suffirais	j'aurais suffi
suffisons	tu suffirais	tu aurais suffi
suffisez	il suffirait	il aurait suffi
	nous suffirions	nous aurions suffi
	vous suffiriez	vous auriez suffi
	ils suffiraient	ils auraient suffi

SUBJUNCTIVE

PRESENT	IMPERFECT	PERFECT
je suffise	je suffisse	j'aie suffi
tu suffises	tu suffisses	tu aies suffi
il suffise	il suffît	il ait suffi
nous suffisions	nous suffissions	nous ayons suffi
vous suffisiez	vous suffissiez	vous ayez suffi
ils suffisent	ils suffissent	ils aient suffi

INFINITIVE	PARTICIPLE	NOTE
PRESENT	**PRESENT**	**circoncire** has the past participle 'circoncis'
suffire	suffisant	
PAST	**PAST**	
avoir suffi	suffi	

SUIVRE to follow

PRESENT
je suis
tu suis
il suit
nous suivons
vous suivez
ils suivent

IMPERFECT
je suivais
tu suivais
il suivait
nous suivions
vous suiviez
ils suivaient

FUTURE
je suivrai
tu suivras
il suivra
nous suivrons
vous suivrez
ils suivront

PAST HISTORIC
je suivis
tu suivis
il suivit
nous suivîmes
vous suivîtes
ils suivirent

PERFECT
j'ai suivi
tu as suivi
il a suivi
nous avons suivi
vous avez suivi
ils ont suivi

PLUPERFECT
j'avais suivi
tu avais suivi
il avait suivi
nous avions suivi
vous aviez suivi
ils avaient suivi

PAST ANTERIOR
j'eus suivi etc

FUTURE PERFECT
j'aurai suivi etc

IMPERATIVE
suis
suivons
suivez

CONDITIONAL

PRESENT
je suivrais
tu suivrais
il suivrait
nous suivrions
vous suivriez
ils suivraient

PAST
j'aurais suivi
tu aurais suivi
il aurait suivi
nous aurions suivi
vous auriez suivi
ils auraient suivi

SUBJUNCTIVE

PRESENT
je suive
tu suives
il suive
nous suivions
vous suiviez
ils suivent

IMPERFECT
je suivisse
tu suivisses
il suivît
nous suivissions
vous suivissiez
ils suivissent

PERFECT
j'aie suivi
tu aies suivi
il ait suivi
nous ayons suivi
vous ayez suivi
ils aient suivi

INFINITIVE

PRESENT
suivre

PAST
avoir suivi

PARTICIPLE

PRESENT
suivant

PAST
suivi

PRESENT	IMPERFECT	FUTURE
je sursois	je sursoyais	je surseoirai
tu sursois	tu sursoyais	tu surseoiras
il sursoit	il sursoyait	il surseoira
nous sursoyons	nous sursoyions	nous surseoirons
vous sursoyez	vous sursoyiez	vous surseoirez
ils sursoient	ils sursoyaient	ils surseoiront
PAST HISTORIC	**PERFECT**	**PLUPERFECT**
je sursis	j'ai sursis	j'avais sursis
tu sursis	tu as sursis	tu avais sursis
il sursit	il a sursis	il avait sursis
nous sursîmes	nous avons sursis	nous avions sursis
vous sursîtes	vous avez sursis	vous aviez sursis
ils sursirent	ils ont sursis	ils avaient sursis
PAST ANTERIOR	**FUTURE PERFECT**	
j'eus sursis etc	j'aurai sursis etc	

IMPERATIVE	CONDITIONAL PRESENT	CONDITIONAL PAST
	je surseoirais	j'aurais sursis
sursois	tu surseoirais	tu aurais sursis
sursoyons	il surseoirait	il aurait sursis
sursoyez	nous surseoirions	nous aurions sursis
	vous surseoiriez	vous auriez sursis
	ils surseoiraient	ils auraient sursis

SUBJUNCTIVE

PRESENT	IMPERFECT	PERFECT
je sursoie	je sursisse	j'aie sursis
tu sursoies	tu sursisses	tu aies sursis
il sursoie	il sursît	il ait sursis
nous sursoyions	nous sursissions	nous ayons sursis
vous sursoyiez	vous sursissiez	vous ayez sursis
ils sursoient	ils sursissent	ils aient sursis

INFINITIVE	PARTICIPLE
PRESENT	**PRESENT**
surseoir	sursoyant
PAST	**PAST**
avoir sursis	sursis

PRESENT	IMPERFECT	FUTURE
je me tais	je me taisais	je me tairai
tu te tais	tu te taisais	tu te tairas
il se tait	il se taisait	il se taira
nous nous taisons	nous nous taisions	nous nous tairons
vous vous taisez	vous vous taisiez	vous vous tairez
ils se taisent	ils se taisaient	ils se tairont
PAST HISTORIC	**PERFECT**	**PLUPERFECT**
je me tus	je me suis tu	je m'étais tu
tu te tus	tu t'es tu	tu t'étais tu
il se tut	il s'est tu	il s'était tu
nous nous tûmes	nous nous sommes tus	nous nous étions tus
vous vous tûtes	vous vous êtes tu(s)	vous vous étiez tu(s)
ils se turent	ils se sont tus	ils s'étaient tus
PAST ANTERIOR	**FUTURE PERFECT**	
je me fus tu etc	je me serai tu etc	

IMPERATIVE	CONDITIONAL PRESENT	CONDITIONAL PAST
	je me tairais	je me serais tu
tais-toi	tu te tairais	tu te serais tu
taisons-nous	il se tairait	il se serait tu
taisez-vous	nous nous tairions	nous nous serions tus
	vous vous tairiez	vous vous seriez tu(s)
	ils se tairaient	ils se seraient tus

SUBJUNCTIVE

PRESENT	IMPERFECT	PERFECT
je me taise	je me tusse	je me sois tu
tu te taises	tu te tusses	tu te sois tu
il se taise	il se tût	il se soit tu
nous nous taisions	nous nous tussions	nous nous soyons tus
vous vous taisiez	vous vous tussiez	vous vous soyez tu(s)
ils se taisent	ils se tussent	ils se soient tus

INFINITIVE	PARTICIPLE
PRESENT	**PRESENT**
se taire	se taisant
PAST	**PAST**
s'être tu	tu

PRESENT	IMPERFECT	FUTURE
je tiens	je tenais	je tiendrai
tu tiens	tu tenais	tu tiendras
il tient	il tenait	il tiendra
nous tenons	nous tenions	nous tiendrons
vous tenez	vous teniez	vous tiendrez
ils tiennent	ils tenaient	ils tiendront
PAST HISTORIC	**PERFECT**	**PLUPERFECT**
je tins	j'ai tenu	j'avais tenu
tu tins	tu as tenu	tu avais tenu
il tint	il a tenu	il avait tenu
nous tînmes	nous avons tenu	nous avions tenu
vous tîntes	vous avez tenu	vous aviez tenu
ils tinrent	ils ont tenu	ils avaient tenu
PAST ANTERIOR	**FUTURE PERFECT**	
j'eus tenu etc	j'aurai tenu etc	

IMPERATIVE	CONDITIONAL	
	PRESENT	**PAST**
tiens	je tiendrais	j'aurais tenu
tenons	tu tiendrais	tu aurais tenu
tenez	il tiendrait	il aurait tenu
	nous tiendrions	nous aurions tenu
	vous tiendriez	vous auriez tenu
	ils tiendraient	ils auraient tenu

SUBJUNCTIVE

PRESENT	IMPERFECT	PERFECT
je tienne	je tinsse	j'aie tenu
tu tiennes	tu tinsses	tu aies tenu
il tienne	il tînt	il ait tenu
nous tenions	nous tinssions	nous ayons tenu
vous teniez	vous tinssiez	vous ayez tenu
ils tiennent	ils tinssent	ils aient tenu

INFINITIVE	PARTICIPLE
PRESENT	**PRESENT**
tenir	tenant
PAST	**PAST**
avoir tenu	tenu

PRESENT	IMPERFECT	FUTURE
je tombe	je tombais	je tomberai
tu tombes	tu tombais	tu tomberas
il tombe	il tombait	il tombera
nous tombons	nous tombions	nous tomberons
vous tombez	vous tombiez	vous tomberez
ils tombent	ils tombaient	ils tomberont

PAST HISTORIC	PERFECT	PLUPERFECT
je tombai	je suis tombé	j'étais tombé
tu tombas	tu es tombé	tu étais tombé
il tomba	il est tombé	il était tombé
nous tombâmes	nous sommes tombés	nous étions tombés
vous tombâtes	vous êtes tombé(s)	vous étiez tombé(s)
ils tombèrent	ils sont tombés	ils étaient tombés

PAST ANTERIOR	FUTURE PERFECT
je fus tombé etc	je serai tombé etc

IMPERATIVE	CONDITIONAL PRESENT	CONDITIONAL PAST
	je tomberais	je serais tombé
tombe	tu tomberais	tu serais tombé
tombons	il tomberait	il serait tombé
tombez	nous tomberions	nous serions tombés
	vous tomberiez	vous seriez tombé(s)
	ils tomberaient	ils seraient tombés

SUBJUNCTIVE

PRESENT	IMPERFECT	PERFECT
je tombe	je tombasse	je sois tombé
tu tombes	tu tombasses	tu sois tombé
il tombe	il tombât	il soit tombé
nous tombions	nous tombassions	nous soyons tombés
vous tombiez	vous tombassiez	vous soyez tombé(s)
ils tombent	ils tombassent	ils soient tombés

INFINITIVE	PARTICIPLE
PRESENT	PRESENT
tomber	tombant
PAST	PAST
être tombé	tombé

TRADUIRE to translate

PRESENT	IMPERFECT	FUTURE
je traduis	je traduisais	je traduirai
tu traduis	tu traduisais	tu traduiras
il traduit	il traduisait	il traduira
nous traduisons	nous traduisions	nous traduirons
vous traduisez	vous traduisiez	vous traduirez
ils traduisent	ils traduisaient	ils traduiront
PAST HISTORIC	**PERFECT**	**PLUPERFECT**
je traduisis	j'ai traduit	j'avais traduit
tu traduisis	tu as traduit	tu avais traduit
il traduisit	il a traduit	il avait traduit
nous traduisîmes	nous avons traduit	nous avions traduit
vous traduisîtes	vous avez traduit	vous aviez traduit
ils traduisirent	ils ont traduit	ils avaient traduit
PAST ANTERIOR	**FUTURE PERFECT**	
j'eus traduit etc	j'aurai traduit etc	

IMPERATIVE	CONDITIONAL PRESENT	CONDITIONAL PAST
	je traduirais	j'aurais traduit
traduis	tu traduirais	tu aurais traduit
traduisons	il traduirait	il aurait traduit
traduisez	nous traduirions	nous aurions traduit
	vous traduiriez	vous auriez traduit
	ils traduiraient	ils auraient traduit

SUBJUNCTIVE

PRESENT	IMPERFECT	PERFECT
je traduise	je traduisisse	j'aie traduit
tu traduises	tu traduisisses	tu aies traduit
il traduise	il traduisît	il ait traduit
nous traduisions	nous traduisissions	nous ayons traduit
vous traduisiez	vous traduisissiez	vous ayez traduit
ils traduisent	ils traduisissent	ils aient traduit

INFINITIVE	PARTICIPLE
PRESENT	**PRESENT**
traduire	traduisant
PAST	**PAST**
avoir traduit	traduit

PRESENT	IMPERFECT	FUTURE
je travaille	je travaillais	je travaillerai
tu travailles	tu travaillais	tu travailleras
il travaille	il travaillait	il travaillera
nous travaillons	nous travaillions	nous travaillerons
vous travaillez	vous travailliez	vous travaillerez
ils travaillent	ils travaillaient	ils travailleront
PAST HISTORIC	**PERFECT**	**PLUPERFECT**
je travaillai	j'ai travaillé	j'avais travaillé
tu travaillas	tu as travaillé	tu avais travaillé
il travailla	il a travaillé	il avait travaillé
nous travaillâmes	nous avons travaillé	nous avions travaillé
vous travaillâtes	vous avez travaillé	vous aviez travaillé
ils travaillèrent	ils ont travaillé	ils avaient travaillé
PAST ANTERIOR	**FUTURE PERFECT**	
j'eus travaillé etc	j'aurai travaillé etc	

IMPERATIVE	CONDITIONAL	
	PRESENT	**PAST**
travaille	je travaillerais	j'aurais travaillé
travaillons	tu travaillerais	tu aurais travaillé
travaillez	il travaillerait	il aurait travaillé
	nous travaillerions	nous aurions travaillé
	vous travailleriez	vous auriez travaillé
	ils travailleraient	ils auraient travaillé

	SUBJUNCTIVE	
PRESENT	**IMPERFECT**	**PERFECT**
je travaille	je travaillasse	j'aie travaillé
tu travailles	tu travaillasses	tu aies travaillé
il travaille	il travaillât	il ait travaillé
nous travaillions	nous travaillassions	nous ayons travaillé
vous travailliez	vous travaillassiez	vous ayez travaillé
ils travaillent	ils travaillassent	ils aient travaillé

INFINITIVE	PARTICIPLE
PRESENT	**PRESENT**
travailler	travaillant
PAST	**PAST**
avoir travaillé	travaillé

PRESENT	IMPERFECT	FUTURE
je tue	je tuais	je tuerai
tu tues	tu tuais	tu tueras
il tue	il tuait	il tuera
nous tuons	nous tuions	nous tuerons
vous tuez	vous tuiez	vous tuerez
ils tuent	ils tuaient	ils tueront
PAST HISTORIC	**PERFECT**	**PLUPERFECT**
je tuai	j'ai tué	j'avais tué
tu tuas	tu as tué	tu avais tué
il tua	il a tué	il avait tué
nous tuâmes	nous avons tué	nous avions tué
vous tuâtes	vous avez tué	vous aviez tué
ils tuèrent	ils ont tué	ils avaient tué
PAST ANTERIOR	**FUTURE PERFECT**	
j'eus tué etc	j'aurai tué etc	

IMPERATIVE	CONDITIONAL	
	PRESENT	PAST
tue	je tuerais	j'aurais tué
tuons	tu tuerais	tu aurais tué
tuez	il tuerait	il aurait tué
	nous tuerions	nous aurions tué
	vous tueriez	vous auriez tué
	ils tueraient	ils auraient tué

	SUBJUNCTIVE	
PRESENT	IMPERFECT	PERFECT
je tue	je tuasse	j'aie tué
tu tues	tu tuasses	tu aies tué
il tue	il tuât	il ait tué
nous tuions	nous tuassions	nous ayons tué
vous tuiez	vous tuassiez	vous ayez tué
ils tuent	ils tuassent	ils aient tué

INFINITIVE	PARTICIPLE
PRESENT	PRESENT
tuer	tuant
PAST	PAST
avoir tué	tué

PRESENT	IMPERFECT	FUTURE
je vaincs	je vainquais	je vaincrai
tu vaincs	tu vainquais	tu vaincras
il vainc	il vainquait	il vaincra
nous vainquons	nous vainquions	nous vaincrons
vous vainquez	vous vainquiez	vous vaincrez
ils vainquent	ils vainquaient	ils vaincront
PAST HISTORIC	**PERFECT**	**PLUPERFECT**
je vainquis	j'ai vaincu	j'avais vaincu
tu vainquis	tu as vaincu	tu avais vaincu
il vainquit	il a vaincu	il avait vaincu
nous vainquîmes	nous avons vaincu	nous avions vaincu
vous vainquîtes	vous avez vaincu	vous aviez vaincu
ils vainquirent	ils ont vaincu	ils avaient vaincu
PAST ANTERIOR	**FUTURE PERFECT**	
j'eus vaincu etc	j'aurai vaincu etc	

IMPERATIVE	CONDITIONAL	
	PRESENT	**PAST**
vaincs	je vaincrais	j'aurais vaincu
vainquons	tu vaincrais	tu aurais vaincu
vainquez	il vaincrait	il aurait vaincu
	nous vaincrions	nous aurions vaincu
	vous vaincriez	vous auriez vaincu
	ils vaincraient	ils auraient vaincu

	SUBJUNCTIVE	
PRESENT	**IMPERFECT**	**PERFECT**
je vainque	je vainquisse	j'aie vaincu
tu vainques	tu vainquisses	tu aies vaincu
il vainque	il vainquît	il ait vaincu
nous vainquions	nous vainquissions	nous ayons vaincu
vous vainquiez	vous vainquissiez	vous ayez vaincu
ils vainquent	ils vainquissent	ils aient vaincu

INFINITIVE	PARTICIPLE
PRESENT	**PRESENT**
vaincre	vainquant
PAST	**PAST**
avoir vaincu	vaincu

PRESENT	IMPERFECT	FUTURE
je vaux	je valais	je vaudrai
tu vaux	tu valais	tu vaudras
il vaut	il valait	il vaudra
nous valons	nous valions	nous vaudrons
vous valez	vous valiez	vous vaudrez
ils valent	ils valaient	ils vaudront
PAST HISTORIC	**PERFECT**	**PLUPERFECT**
je valus	j'ai valu	j'avais valu
tu valus	tu as valu	tu avais valu
il valut	il a valu	il avait valu
nous valûmes	nous avons valu	nous avions valu
vous valûtes	vous avez valu	vous aviez valu
ils valurent	ils ont valu	ils avaient valu
PAST ANTERIOR	**FUTURE PERFECT**	
j'eus valu etc	j'aurai valu etc	

IMPERATIVE	CONDITIONAL PRESENT	CONDITIONAL PAST
vaux	je vaudrais	j'aurais valu
valons	tu vaudrais	tu aurais valu
valez	il vaudrait	il aurait valu
	nous vaudrions	nous aurions valu
	vous vaudriez	vous auriez valu
	ils vaudraient	ils auraient valu

SUBJUNCTIVE

PRESENT	IMPERFECT	PERFECT
je vaille	je valusse	j'aie valu
tu vailles	tu valusses	tu aies valu
il vaille	il valût	il ait valu
nous valions	nous valussions	nous ayons valu
vous valiez	vous valussiez	vous ayez valu
ils vaillent	ils valussent	ils aient valu

INFINITIVE	PARTICIPLE
PRESENT	**PRESENT**
valoir	valant
PAST	**PAST**
avoir valu	valu

PRESENT	IMPERFECT	FUTURE
je vends	je vendais	je vendrai
tu vends	tu vendais	tu vendras
il vend	il vendait	il vendra
nous vendons	nous vendions	nous vendrons
vous vendez	vous vendiez	vous vendrez
ils vendent	ils vendaient	ils vendront
PAST HISTORIC	**PERFECT**	**PLUPERFECT**
je vendis	j'ai vendu	j'avais vendu
tu vendis	tu as vendu	tu avais vendu
il vendit	il a vendu	il avait vendu
nous vendîmes	nous avons vendu	nous avions vendu
vous vendîtes	vous avez vendu	vous aviez vendu
ils vendirent	ils ont vendu	ils avaient vendu
PAST ANTERIOR	**FUTURE PERFECT**	
j'eus vendu etc	j'aurai vendu etc	

IMPERATIVE	CONDITIONAL	
	PRESENT	**PAST**
vends	je vendrais	j'aurais vendu
vendons	tu vendrais	tu aurais vendu
vendez	il vendrait	il aurait vendu
	nous vendrions	nous aurions vendu
	vous vendriez	vous auriez vendu
	ils vendraient	ils auraient vendu

	SUBJUNCTIVE	
PRESENT	**IMPERFECT**	**PERFECT**
je vende	je vendisse	j'aie vendu
tu vendes	tu vendisses	tu aies vendu
il vende	il vendît	il ait vendu
nous vendions	nous vendissions	nous ayons vendu
vous vendiez	vous vendissiez	vous ayez vendu
ils vendent	ils vendissent	ils aient vendu

INFINITIVE	PARTICIPLE
PRESENT	**PRESENT**
vendre	vendant
PAST	**PAST**
avoir vendu	vendu

PRESENT	IMPERFECT	FUTURE
je viens	je venais	je viendrai
tu viens	tu venais	tu viendras
il vient	il venait	il viendra
nous venons	nous venions	nous viendrons
vous venez	vous veniez	vous viendrez
ils viennent	ils venaient	ils viendront
PAST HISTORIC	**PERFECT**	**PLUPERFECT**
je vins	je suis venu	j'étais venu
tu vins	tu es venu	tu étais venu
il vint	il est venu	il était venu
nous vînmes	nous sommes venus	nous étions venus
vous vîntes	vous êtes venu(s)	vous étiez venu(s)
ils vinrent	ils sont venus	ils étaient venus
PAST ANTERIOR	**FUTURE PERFECT**	
je fus venu etc	je serai venu etc	

IMPERATIVE	CONDITIONAL PRESENT	CONDITIONAL PAST
	je viendrais	je serais venu
viens	tu viendrais	tu serais venu
venons	il viendrait	il serait venu
venez	nous viendrions	nous serions venus
	vous viendriez	vous seriez venu(s)
	ils viendraient	ils seraient venus

SUBJUNCTIVE

PRESENT	IMPERFECT	PERFECT
je vienne	je vinsse	je sois venu
tu viennes	tu vinsses	tu sois venu
il vienne	il vînt	il soit venu
nous venions	nous vinssions	nous soyons venus
vous veniez	vous vinssiez	vous soyez venu(s)
ils viennent	ils vinssent	ils soient venus

INFINITIVE	PARTICIPLE
PRESENT	**PRESENT**
venir	venant
PAST	**PAST**
être venu	venu

PRESENT	IMPERFECT	FUTURE
je vêts	je vêtais	je vêtirai
tu vêts	tu vêtais	tu vêtiras
il vêt	il vêtait	il vêtira
nous vêtons	nous vêtions	nous vêtirons
vous vêtez	vous vêtiez	vous vêtirez
ils vêtent	ils vêtaient	ils vêtiront
PAST HISTORIC	**PERFECT**	**PLUPERFECT**
je vêtis	j'ai vêtu	j'avais vêtu
tu vêtis	tu as vêtu	tu avais vêtu
il vêtit	il a vêtu	il avait vêtu
nous vêtîmes	nous avons vêtu	nous avions vêtu
vous vêtîtes	vous avez vêtu	vous aviez vêtu
ils vêtirent	ils ont vêtu	ils avaient vêtu
PAST ANTERIOR	**FUTURE PERFECT**	
j'eus vêtu etc	j'aurai vêtu etc	

IMPERATIVE	CONDITIONAL PRESENT	CONDITIONAL PAST
	je vêtirais	j'aurais vêtu
vêts	tu vêtirais	tu aurais vêtu
vêtons	il vêtirait	il aurait vêtu
vêtez	nous vêtirions	nous aurions vêtu
	vous vêtiriez	vous auriez vêtu
	ils vêtiraient	ils auraient vêtu

SUBJUNCTIVE

PRESENT	IMPERFECT	PERFECT
je vête	je vêtisse	j'aie vêtu
tu vêtes	tu vêtisses	tu aies vêtu
il vête	il vêtît	il ait vêtu
nous vêtions	nous vêtissions	nous ayons vêtu
vous vêtiez	vous vêtissiez	vous ayez vêtu
ils vêtent	ils vêtissent	ils aient vêtu

INFINITIVE	PARTICIPLE
PRESENT	**PRESENT**
vêtir	vêtant
PAST	**PAST**
avoir vêtu	vêtu

PRESENT	IMPERFECT	FUTURE
je vis	je vivais	je vivrai
tu vis	tu vivais	tu vivras
il vit	il vivait	il vivra
nous vivons	nous vivions	nous vivrons
vous vivez	vous viviez	vous vivrez
ils vivent	ils vivaient	ils vivront
PAST HISTORIC	**PERFECT**	**PLUPERFECT**
je vécus	j'ai vécu	j'avais vécu
tu vécus	tu as vécu	tu avais vécu
il vécut	il a vécu	il avait vécu
nous vécûmes	nous avons vécu	nous avions vécu
vous vécûtes	vous avez vécu	vous aviez vécu
ils vécurent	ils ont vécu	ils avaient vécu
PAST ANTERIOR	**FUTURE PERFECT**	
j'eus vécu etc	j'aurai vécu etc	

IMPERATIVE	CONDITIONAL	
	PRESENT	**PAST**
vis	je vivrais	j'aurais vécu
vivons	tu vivrais	tu aurais vécu
vivez	il vivrait	il aurait vécu
	nous vivrions	nous aurions vécu
	vous vivriez	vous auriez vécu
	ils vivraient	ils auraient vécu

	SUBJUNCTIVE	
PRESENT	**IMPERFECT**	**PERFECT**
je vive	je vécusse	j'aie vécu
tu vives	tu vécusses	tu aies vécu
il vive	il vécût	il ait vécu
nous vivions	nous vécussions	nous ayons vécu
vous viviez	vous vécussiez	vous ayez vécu
ils vivent	ils vécussent	ils aient vécu

INFINITIVE	PARTICIPLE
PRESENT	**PRESENT**
vivre	vivant
PAST	**PAST**
avoir vécu	vécu

PRESENT	IMPERFECT	FUTURE
je vois	je voyais	je verrai
tu vois	tu voyais	tu verras
il voit	il voyait	il verra
nous voyons	nous voyions	nous verrons
vous voyez	vous voyiez	vous verrez
ils voient	ils voyaient	ils verront
PAST HISTORIC	**PERFECT**	**PLUPERFECT**
je vis	j'ai vu	j'avais vu
tu vis	tu as vu	tu avais vu
il vit	il a vu	il avait vu
nous vîmes	nous avons vu	nous avions vu
vous vîtes	vous avez vu	vous aviez vu
ils virent	ils ont vu	ils avaient vu
PAST ANTERIOR	**FUTURE PERFECT**	
j'eus vu etc	j'aurai vu etc	

IMPERATIVE	CONDITIONAL	
	PRESENT	**PAST**
vois	je verrais	j'aurais vu
voyons	tu verrais	tu aurais vu
voyez	il verrait	il aurait vu
	nous verrions	nous aurions vu
	vous verriez	vous auriez vu
	ils verraient	ils auraient vu

	SUBJUNCTIVE	
PRESENT	**IMPERFECT**	**PERFECT**
je voie	je visse	j'aie vu
tu voies	tu visses	tu aies vu
il voie	il vît	il ait vu
nous voyions	nous vissions	nous ayons vu
vous voyiez	vous vissiez	vous ayez vu
ils voient	ils vissent	ils aient vu

INFINITIVE	PARTICIPLE
PRESENT	**PRESENT**
voir	voyant
PAST	**PAST**
avoir vu	vu

PRESENT
je veux
tu veux
il veut
nous voulons
vous voulez
ils veulent

IMPERFECT
je voulais
tu voulais
il voulait
nous voulions
vous vouliez
ils voulaient

FUTURE
je voudrai
tu voudras
il voudra
nous voudrons
vous voudrez
ils voudront

PAST HISTORIC
je voulus
tu voulus
il voulut
nous voulûmes
vous voulûtes
ils voulurent

PERFECT
j'ai voulu
tu as voulu
il a voulu
nous avons voulu
vous avez voulu
ils ont voulu

PLUPERFECT
j'avais voulu
tu avais voulu
il avait voulu
nous avions voulu
vous aviez voulu
ils avaient voulu

PAST ANTERIOR
j'eus voulu etc

FUTURE PERFECT
j'aurai voulu etc

IMPERATIVE
veuille
veuillons
veuillez

CONDITIONAL

PRESENT
je voudrais
tu voudrais
il voudrait
nous voudrions
vous voudriez
ils voudraient

PAST
j'aurais voulu
tu aurais voulu
il aurait voulu
nous aurions voulu
vous auriez voulu
ils auraient voulu

SUBJUNCTIVE

PRESENT
je veuille
tu veuilles
il veuille
nous voulions
vous vouliez
ils veuillent

IMPERFECT
je voulusse
tu voulusses
il voulût
nous voulussions
vous voulussiez
ils voulussent

PERFECT
j'aie voulu
tu aies voulu
il ait voulu
nous ayons voulu
vous ayez voulu
ils aient voulu

INFINITIVE

PRESENT
vouloir

PAST
avoir voulu

PARTICIPLE

PRESENT
voulant

PAST
voulu

ACCROIRE to believe

INFINITIVE
PRESENT
accroire

APPAROIR to appear

PRESENT
il appert

INFINITIVE
PRESENT
apparoir

OUÏR to hear

INFINITIVE	PARTICIPLE
PRESENT	**PAST**
ouïr	ouï

INDEX OF FRENCH VERBS

The verbs given in full in the tables on the preceding pages are used as models for all other French verbs given in this index. The number in the index is that of the corresponding verb table.

Bold type denotes a verb that is given as a model itself.

A second number in brackets refers to a reflexive verb model or to the model for a verb starting with an 'h' (indicating whether it is aspirated or not).

An N in brackets refers to a footnote in the model verb table.

Reflexive verbs are listed alphabetically under the simple verb form and the reflexive pronoun (se or s') is given in brackets.

The few cases where a verb does not have the same auxiliary as its model are indicated in the footnotes .

abaisser 154
abandonner 67
abattre 25
abêtir 92
abîmer 8
abolir 92
abonder 8
abonner (s') 118
aborder 8
aboutir 92
aboyer 129
abréger 163
abreuver 8
abriter 8
abrutir 92
absenter (s') 118
absorber 8
absoudre 65
abstenir (s') 192
abstraire 66
abuser 8
accabler 8
accaparer 8
accéder 29
accélérer 156
accepter 8
acclamer 8
accommoder 8
accompagner 97
accomplir 92
accorder 8
accoucher 8
accouder (s') 118
accourir 43 (N)
accoutumer 8
accrocher 8
accroire 211
accroître 1
accroupir (s') 87
accueillir 2
accumuler 8
accuser 8
acharner (s') 118
acheminer 8
acheter 3
achever 73
acquérir 4
acquiescer 147
acquitter 8
actionner 67
activer 8
adapter 8
additionner 67
adhérer 156
adjoindre 109
admettre 121
administrer 8
admirer 8
adonner (s') 118
adopter 8
adorer 8
adosser 154
adoucir 92
adresser 154
advenir 5
aérer 8
affaiblir 6
affairer (s') 118
affaisser (s') 118
affamer 8
affecter 8
affermir 92
afficher 8
affirmer 8
affliger 111

atteler 14
attendre 22
attendrir 92
atténuer 202
atterrir 92
attirer 8
attraper 8
attribuer 202
augmenter 8
ausculter 8
autoriser 8
avachir (s') 87
avaler 8
avancer 23
avantager 111
aventurer (s') 118
avérer (s') 156 (118)
avertir 92
aveugler 8
avilir 92
aviser 8
aviver 8
avoir 24
avorter 8
avouer 110

bâcler 31
bafouer 110
bafouiller 93
bagarrer (se) 118
baigner 97
bâiller 201
bâillonner 67
baiser 31
baisser 154
balader (se) 118
balancer 112
balayer 140
balbutier 47
baliser 31
balloter 31
bannir 92
baptiser 31
baratiner 31
barbouiller 93
barioler 31
barrer 31
barricader 31
basculer 31
baser 31
batailler 201
batifoler 31
bâtir 92
battre 25
bavarder 31
baver 31
béer 46
bégayer 140
bêler 31
bénéficier 15
bénir 92
bercer 147
berner 31
beugler 31
beurrer 31
biaiser 31
bichonner 67
biffer 31
blaguer 128
blâmer 31
blanchir 92
blaser 31
blasphémer 71
blêmir 92
blesser 154
bloquer 103
blottir (se) 87
boire 26
boiter 31
bombarder 31
bondir 92
bonifier 47
border 31
borner 31
boucher 31
boucler 31
bouder 31
bouffer 31
bouffir 92
bouger 111
bouillir 27
bouleverser 31
bourdonner 67
bourrer 31
boursouffler 31
bousculer 31
boutonner 67
braconner 67
brailler 201
braire 66 (N)
brancher 31
brandir 92
branler 31
braquer 103
brasser 154
braver 31
bredouiller 93
breveter 108
bricoler 31
brider 31
briguer 128
briller 28
brimer 31
briser 31
broder 31
broncher 31
bronzer 31
brosser 154
brouiller 93
brouter 31
broyer 129
brûler 31
brunir 92
brusquer 103
brutaliser 31
buter 31
butiner 31

cabrer 31
cacher 31
cadrer 31
cajoler 31
calculer 31
caler 31
calmer 31
calomnier 47
calquer 103
cambrioler 31

décommander 31
déconcerter 31
déconseiller 41
décontracter (se) 118
décorer 31
découdre 42
découler 31
découper 31
décourager 111
découvrir 53
décréter 35
décrier 47
décrire 54
décrocher 31
décroître 1
dédaigner 97
dédicacer 147
dédier 47
dédire (se) 105 (197)
dédommager 111
dédouaner 31
dédoubler 31
déduire 200
défaillir 55
défaire 90
défalquer 103
défavoriser 31
défendre 56
déférer 156
déferler 31
déficeler 14
défier 47
défigurer 31
défiler 31
définir 92
défoncer 11
déformer 31
défouler (se) 118
défraîchir 92
défricher 31
dégager 111
dégainer 31
dégauchir 92
dégeler 142
dégénérer 156
dégonfler 31
dégourdir 92
dégoûter 31
dégrader 31
dégringoler 31
dégriser 31
dégrossir 92
déguerpir 92
déguiser 31
déguster 31
déjeuner 31
déjouer 110
délaisser 154
délayer 140
délecter 31
déléguer 113
délibérer 156
délier 47
délimiter 31
délirer 31
délivrer 31
déloger 111
demander 31
démanger 116
démanteler 142
démaquiller 28
démarquer 103
démarrer 31
démasquer 103
démêler 31
déménager 111
démener (se) 119 (118)
démentir 120
démettre 121
demeurer 31 (N)
démissionner 67
démolir 92
démonter 57
démontrer 31
démoraliser 31
démouler 31
démunir 92
dénaturer 31
dénicher 31
dénier 47
dénigrer 31
dénombrer 31
dénoncer 11
dénouer 110
dépanner 31
départager 111
départir (se) 76
dépasser 154
dépayser 31
dépecer 58
dépêcher 31
dépeindre 141
dépendre 205
dépenser 31
dépérir 92
dépister 31
déplacer 147
déplaire 148
déplier 47
déplorer 31
déployer 129
dépolir 92
déposer 31
dépouiller 93
dépoussiérer 156
déprécier 15
déprimer 31
déraciner 31
dérailler 201
déranger 116
déraper 31
dérégler 168
dérider 31
dériver 31
dérober 31
déroger 111
dérouler 31
dérouter 31
désaccoutumer 31
désagréger 163
désaltérer 156
désamorcer 147
désapprendre 16
désapprouver 31
désarmer 31
désavantager 111
désavouer 110
descendre 59

ENGLISH-FRENCH INDEX

The following is an index of the most common English verbs and their main translations. Note that the correct translation for the English verb depends entirely on the context in which the verb is used and the user should consult a dictionary if in any doubt.

The verbs given in full in the tables on the preceding pages are used as models for all the French verbs given in this index. The number in the index is that of the corresponding verb table.

Bold type denotes a verb that is given as a model itself.

A second number in brackets refers to a reflexive verb model or to the model for a verb starting with an 'h' (indicating whether it is aspirated or not).

An N in brackets refers to a footnote in the model verb table.

announce **annoncer 11**
annoy agacer 147, contrarier 47, embêter 8
answer **répondre 174**
anticipate anticiper 8, **prévoir 160**
apologize excuser (s') 118
appal choquer 103
appear apparaître 136, figurer 31, **paraître 136**
applaud applaudir 92
apply appliquer 103, étaler 8
apply for solliciter 31
appoint affecter 8, nommer 31
appreciate **apprécier 15**
approach aborder 8, approcher 8
approve (of) approuver 8
argue discuter 31, disputer (se) 31 (118)
arise survenir 206
arm armer 8
arouse exciter 8, provoquer 103
arrange arranger 116, disposer 31
arrest appréhender 8, arrêter 8
arrive arriver 19
ask demander 31
aspire aspirer 8
assault agresser 154, **assaillir 20**
assemble assembler 8, **monter 122**
assert affirmer 8, revendiquer 103
assess estimer 8, évaluer 202
assign affecter 8, assigner 97
assist aider 8
associate associer 15
assume assumer 8, présumer 31
assure assurer 8
astound ébahir 82
attack agresser 154, attaquer 103
attempt tenter 31
attend assister 8, **suivre 195**
attract attirer 8
authorize accorder 8, autoriser 8
avert écarter 8
avoid éviter 8
awake éveiller (s') 41 (118), réveiller (se) 41 (118)
award accorder 8, décerner 31
axe supprimer 31
back **appuyer 17**, financer 112
balance équilibrer 8
ban **interdire 105**
bang cogner 97
baptize baptiser 31
bar barrer 31, exclure 37
bare **découvrir 53**
bark aboyer 129
base baser 31
bath baigner (se) 97 (118)
bathe baigner (se) 97 (118), laver 31
be **être 85**
bear porter 31, supporter 31
beat **battre 25**, fouetter 31
become **devenir 61**
beg mendier 47, prier 47
begin **commencer 34**
believe croire 48
belong **appartenir 13**
bend courber 31, plier 47
benefit bénéficier 15
bet parier 47
betray trahir 82
bind relier 47
bite **mordre 123**
blame blâmer 31, reprocher 31
blare beugler 31
blaze flamber 31
bleed saigner 97
blend fondre 174
bless bénir 92
blind aveugler 8
blink cligner 97
block bloquer 103, encombrer 8
block off barrer 31
block up boucher 31
blow souffler 31
blow up gonfler 31, sauter 31
blush rougir 7
boil **bouillir 27**
bolt verrouiller 93
bomb bombarder 31
book réserver 31
boost relancer 112
border on côtoyer 129
bore **ennuyer 78**, forer 31
born (be) **naître 127**
borrow emprunter 8
bother **ennuyer 78**, gêner 31
bounce rebondir 92
bow saluer 202
brace raidir 92

brake freiner 31
brave braver 31
break briser 31, casser 154, **rompre 181**
break out éclater 8
break up démanteler 142, désintégrer 104, rompre 181
breathe respirer 31
breathe in inspirer 8
breathe out expirer 8
bribe corrompre 181
bridle brider 31
brighten (up) égayer 140, éclaircir (s') 92 (118)
bring amener 119, apporter 8
bring about entraîner 8, provoquer 103
bring back ramener 119, rapporter 31
bring forward décaler 31
bring out **sortir 191**
bring round ranimer 31
bring up **élever 73**, **monter 122**
broadcast diffuser 31, émettre 121
broaden élargir 7
browse feuilleter 108
bruise meurtrir 92
brush brosser 154, effleurer 8
buckle boucler 31
build bâtir 92, construire 60
bully brimer 31, brutaliser 31
bump into rencontrer 31, **rentrer 172**
burgle cambrioler 31
burn brûler 31
burst crever 73, éclater 8
bury ensevelir 92, enterrer 188
butter beurrer 31
button boutonner 67
buy **acheter 3**
buzz bourdonner 67

calculate calculer 31
call **appeler 14**
call back rappeler 14
call off annuler 8
calm (down) calmer (se) 31 (118)
camp camper 31
campaign militer 31
can **pouvoir 155**
cancel annuler 8
capsize chavirer 31
capture capter 31, capturer 31
carry porter 31, transporter 31
carry away entraîner 8, emporter 8
carry off emporter 8
carry on continuer 202
carry out accomplir 92, exécuter 8
carve découper 31, graver 31
cash encaisser 154, toucher 31
cast **jeter 108**, projeter 108
catch attraper 8, **prendre 157**
catch up rattraper 31
cause causer 31, provoquer 103
cease cesser 154
celebrate **célébrer 30**, fêter 31
certify certifier 47, constater 31
chain enchaîner 8
chair présider 31
challenge défier 47
change changer 116
charge charger 111, inculper 8
charm charmer 31, séduire 200
chase poursuivre 195
chat bavarder 31, causer 31
cheat tricher 31
check contrôler 31, vérifier 47
check in enregistrer 8
cheer acclamer 8
cheer up égayer 140, remonter 122
cherish chérir 92
chew mâcher 31, mastiquer 103
chill glacer 147, rafraîchir 92
chisel ciseler 142
choke suffoquer 103
choose choisir 92
chop (up) hacher 101
circle encercler 8
circulate circuler 31
claim prétendre 205, réclamer 31
clamp immobiliser 8, **serrer 188**
clap applaudir 92
classify classer 154, classifier 47
clean **nettoyer 129**
clear dégager 111, éclaircir 92
clear off décamper 31
clench **serrer 188**
click claquer 103
climb grimper 31, **monter 122**
cling to accrocher (s') 118, cramponner (se) 118
clip couper 31, rogner 97
close fermer 31

cram	bourrer 31
crash (into)	percuter 31, **rentrer 172**
crawl	ramper 31
creak	grincer 147
crease	froisser 154
create	**créer 46**
credit	créditer 31
criticize	critiquer 103
crop	tailler 201
crop up	surgir 92
cross	croiser 31, traverser 31
cross out	rayer 140
crouch	accroupir (s') 87
crown	couronner 67
crucify	crucifier 47
crumble	crouler 31, écrouler (s') 118
crumple	froisser 154
crunch	croquer 103
crush	broyer 129, écraser 8
cry	**crier 47**, pleurer 31
cuddle	cajoler 31
curb	brider 31, freiner 31
cure	guérir 92
curl	boucler 31, friser 31
curse	**maudire 117**
cut	couper 31, réduire 200
cut down	abréger 163, réduire 200
cut out	supprimer 31, tailler 201
cut up	découper 31
damage	abîmer 8
dance	danser 31
dare	oser 8
darken	assombrir 92, obscurcir 92
dash	précipiter (se) 31 (118)
date	dater 31
dawdle	traîner 31
daze	abrutir 92, étourdir 92
dazzle	éblouir 92
deafen	assourdir 92
deal with	traiter 31, occuper de (s') 118
debate	débattre 25
debit	débiter 31
decay	dépérir 92, pourrir 92
deceive	abuser 8, tromper 31
decide	décider 31
declare	déclarer 31
decline	décliner 31
decorate	décorer 31, orner 8
decrease	décroître 1, diminuer 202
dedicate	dédicacer 147, dédier 47
deduce	déduire 200
deduct	déduire 200
defeat	**vaincre 203**
defend	**défendre 56**, soutenir 198
defer	différer 156
define	définir 92, délimiter 31
deflate	dégonfler 31
defrost	dégeler 142
defy	braver 31, défier 47
degrade	avilir 92, dégrader 31
delay	retarder 31, tarder 31
delete	effacer 147, supprimer 31
deliberate	délibérer 156
delight	ravir 92, réjouir 92
deliver	distribuer 202, livrer 31
demand	exiger 111, réclamer 31
demolish	démolir 92
demonstrate	démontrer 31
demoralize	démoraliser 31
demote	dégrader 31, rétrograder 31
denounce	dénoncer 11
deny	démentir 120, nier 47
depart	**partir 137**
depend	dépendre 205
deport	expulser 8
depress	déprimer 31
deprive	priver 31
derive	dériver 31
describe	**décrire 54**
desert	abandonner 67, délaisser 154
deserve	mériter 31
design	concevoir 166, dessiner 31
designate	désigner 97
desire	désirer 31
despair	désespérer 84
despise	dédaigner 97, mépriser 31
destroy	anéantir 92, **détruire 60**
detach	détacher 31
detail	détailler 201
detain	retenir 198
detect	détecter 31
determine	déterminer 31
detest	détester 31
devastate	dévaster 31
develop	développer 31
devise	imaginer 8
devote	dévouer 118, consacrer 31

dial	composer 31
dictate	dicter 31
die	décéder 29 (N), **mourir 125**
die out	disparaître 136
differ	différer 156
dig	creuser 31
digest	digérer 156
digress	dévier 47
dilute	diluer 202
dim	atténuer 202, baisser 154
diminish	amoindrir 92
dine	dîner 31
dip	tremper 31
direct	diriger 111, orienter 8
dirty	salir 92, souiller 93
disable	handicaper 101
disallow	rejeter 108
disappear	disparaître 136
disappoint	décevoir 166
disapprove of	désapprouver 31
discern	discerner 31
discharge	libérer 156
disclose	divulguer 128
disconnect	déboîter 31, débrancher 31
discourage	décourager 111
discover	**découvrir 53**
discuss	débattre 25, discuter 31
disfigure	défigurer 31
disgrace	déshonorer 31
disguise	déguiser 31
disgust	dégoûter 31, écœurer 8
disinfect	désinfecter 31
disintegrate	désintégrer 104
dislocate	déboîter 31
dismay	consterner 31
dismiss	congédier 47, licencier 15, renvoyer 83
disobey	désobéir 131
disorientate	désorienter 31
disown	désavouer 110, renier 47
dispatch	dépêcher 31, expédier 86
dispel	dissiper 31
dispense	administrer 8, dispenser 31
display	afficher 8, exposer 8
displease	déplaire 148, mécontenter 31
dispose of	débarrasser de (se) 154 (118)
dispute	contester 31
disqualify	éliminer 8
disrupt	perturber 31
dissolve	**dissoudre 65**
dissuade	dissuader 31
distinguish	distinguer 128
distort	déformer (se) 31 (118)
distract	**distraire 66**
distress	affliger 111, bouleverser 31
distribute	distribuer 202
disturb	déranger 116, troubler 31
dive	**plonger 150**
diversify	diversifier 47
divert	détourner 31, dévier 47
divide	diviser 31, partager 111
divorce	divorcer 147
divulge	divulguer 128
do	**faire 90**
dominate	dominer 31
double	doubler 31
doubt	douter 31
downgrade	déclasser 154, rétrograder 31
download	télécharger 111
doze	sommeiller 41
doze off	assoupir (s') 87
draft	ébaucher 8, rédiger 111
drag	traîner 31
drain	égoutter 8
draw	dessiner 31, tirer 31
draw up	dresser 154, rédiger 111
dread	redouter 31
dream	rêver 31
dress	habiller 28 (100), **vêtir 207**
dress up	déguiser 31
drift	dériver 31
drill	forer 31, percer 147
drink	**boire 26**
drive	**conduire 38**, **pousser 154**
drop	laisser tomber 154
drop off	déposer 31, **endormir (s') 76**
drop out	abandonner 67
drown	noyer 129
drug	droguer 128
dry	**sécher 184**
dry up	dessécher 184, tarir 92
dull	amortir 92, engourdir 92
dump	décharger 111, déverser 31
dupe	duper 31
dust	dépoussiérer 156
dye	teindre 141

fall through	échouer 110
fan	éventer 8
farm	cultiver 31, exploiter 8
fascinate	fasciner 31
fast	jeûner 31
fasten	attacher 8
favour	favoriser 31
fear	**craindre 45**
feed	alimenter 8, nourrir 92
feel	éprouver 8, **sentir 186**
feign	feindre 141, simuler 31
fiddle	tripoter 31, trafiquer 103, truquer 103
fight	combattre 25, disputer 31, lutter 31
figure	figurer 31
file	classer 154, limer 31
fill	charger 111, remplir 92
fill in	boucher 31, combler 31, remplir 92
fill out	remplir 92
film	filmer 31
finalize	**conclure 37**
finance	financer 112
find	trouver 31
finish	**finir 92**, terminer 31
fire	tirer 31, virer 31
fish	pêcher 31
fit	ajuster 8
fit in	**rentrer 172**
fix	fixer 31, réparer 31
flash	clignoter 31
flatten	aplatir 92
flatter	flatter 31
flavour	parfumer 31
flicker	trembler 31, vaciller 28
float	flotter 31
flood	inonder 8
flourish	fleurir 92
flow	couler 31
flower	fleurir 92
flutter	**battre 25**, palpiter 31
fly	voler 31
fly away	envoler (s') 118
focus	concentrer 31
fold	plier 47
follow	**suivre 195**
fool	duper 31, tromper 31
forbid	**défendre 56, interdire 105**
force	contraindre 45, forcer 147, obliger 111
forecast	anticiper 8, **prévoir 160**
forge	contrefaire 90, forger 111
forget	oublier 86
forgive	pardonner 67
form	constituer 202, former 31
found	fonder 31
frame	cadrer 31, encadrer 8
free	libérer 156
freeze	geler 142
frequent	fréquenter 31
freshen	rafraîchir 92
frighten	effrayer 140
frustrate	frustrer 31
fry	**frire 95**
fulfil	réaliser 31
function	fonctionner 67
furnish	meubler 31
fuss	agiter (s') 7 (118)
gain	**gagner 97**
gamble	**jouer 110**
gasp	haleter 3 (101)
gather	ramasser 154, rassembler (se) 31 (118)
gaze at	contempler 31
generate	générer 156
get	**avoir 24**, **obtenir 132**, procurer 31, **prendre 157**, **recevoir 166**
get back	récupérer 156, **retourner 177**
get out	**sortir 191**
get together	réunir (se) 92 (118)
give	**donner 67**, **offrir 133**
give back	**rendre 171**
give out	émettre 121
give up	abandonner 67, renoncer 11
give way	**céder 29**
glide	glisser 154
glisten	luire 130
gloat	exulter 8
glow	luire 130
gnaw	ronger 150
go	**aller 9**, **partir 137**
go away	**aller (s'en) 10**, partir 137
go by	**passer 139**
go down	**descendre 59**

include **comprendre 36**, **inclure 102**
increase **accroître 1**, augmenter 8
incur encourir 43
indicate **indiquer 103**
induce induire 107
infect infecter 8
infer inférer 156
infiltrate infiltrer 8
inflate gonfler 31
inflict infliger 111
influence influencer 34
inform aviser 8, informer 8, renseigner 97
inhabit peupler 31
inhale aspirer 8, inhaler 8
inherit hériter 100
inject injecter 8
injure blesser 154
inquire enquérir (s') 4 (87), renseigner (se) 97 (118)
insert insérer 156
insist insister 8
inspect examiner 8, inspecter 8
inspire inspirer 8
install installer 8
insult injurier 86, insulter 8
integrate **intégrer 104**
interest intéresser 154
interfere immiscer (s') 147 (118), mêler (se) 31 (118)
interpret interpréter 35
interrupt interrompre 181
intimidate intimider 8
intrigue intriguer 128
introduce **introduire 107**, présenter 31
intrude déranger 116
invade **envahir 82**
invent inventer 8
invert inverser 8, renverser 31
invest investir 92
investigate enquêter 8
invigorate vivifier 47
invite inviter 8
invoice facturer 31
involve impliquer 103
iron repasser 139 (N)
irritate irriter 8
isolate isoler 8
issue émettre 121
itch démanger 116

jam bloquer 103, coincer 147
join **joindre 109**, rejoindre 109, unir 92
joke plaisanter 31, rigoler 31
judge **juger 111**
jump sauter 31
jump over franchir 92
justify justifier 47

keep conserver 31, garder 31, maintenir 198
keep up soutenir 198
kill **tuer 202**
kiss embrasser 154
kneel (down) agenouiller (s') 93 (118)
knit tricoter 31
knock frapper 31
knock down abattre 25
knock over culbuter 31, renverser 31
knot nouer 110
know **connaître 40**, **savoir 183**

lace (up) lacer 147
land atterrir 92, retomber 199
last durer 31
laugh rigoler 31, **rire 180**
launch **lancer 112**
lay **mettre 121**, pondre 174, poser 31
lay down poser 31
lay off débaucher 31
lead **conduire 38**, diriger 111, **mener 119**
leak couler 31
lean **adosser 154**, appuyer 17
lean over pencher 31
leap bondir 92, sauter 31
learn **apprendre 16**
leave laisser 154, **partir 137**, quitter 31
leave out omettre 121
lend prêter 31
lengthen allonger 150, rallonger 150
lessen **affaiblir 6**
let laisser 154
let down décevoir 166, dégonfler 31, rallonger 150

let go of — lâcher 31
let in — admettre 121
let out — élargir 7, lâcher 31
let up — relâcher 31
level — aplanir 92, niveler 14
libel — calomnier 47
liberate — libérer 156
lick — lécher 31
lie — allonger (s') 150 (118), coucher (se) 31 (118), **mentir 120**
lie down — allonger (s') 150 (118), coucher (se) 31 (118)
lift — lever 73, soulever 73
lift up — soulever 73
light — allumer 8, éclairer 8
light up — illuminer 8
lighten — alléger 163, éclaircir 92
like — **aimer 8**, **apprécier 15**
limit — limiter 31
limp — boiter 31
line — border 31, garnir 92
link — lier 47, relier 47
listen — écouter 8
live — habiter 100, **vivre 208**
liven up — animer 8, égayer 140
load — charger 111
loan — prêter 31
locate — repérer 156, situer 202
lock — verrouiller 93
look — regarder 31
look after — garder 31, occuper de (s') 8 (118)
look for — chercher 31, rechercher 31
loosen — desserrer 188, relâcher 31
lose — **perdre 144**
love — **aimer 8**
lower — baisser 154, **descendre 59**

machine — usiner 8
mail — **envoyer 83**
maintain — conserver 31, entretenir 198, maintenir 198
make — fabriquer 103, **faire 90**
make out — distinguer 128
make up — constituer 202, inventer 8, maquiller 28, préparer 31
make up for — compenser 31
manage — administrer 8, débrouiller (se) 93 (118), diriger 111, gérer 156
manufacture — fabriquer 103, manufacturer 31
march — défiler 31, marcher 31
mark — corriger 111, marquer 103
mark down — démarquer 103
marry — épouser 8, marier 47
mask — masquer 103
master — dominer 31, maîtriser 31
match — apparier 86, assortir 92
materialize — matérialiser 31
matter — compter 31, importer 8
mature — mûrir 92
mean — signifier 47
measure — mesurer 31
meet — rejoindre 109, rencontrer 31, retrouver 31
melt — fondre 174
mend — raccommoder 31, réparer 31
mention — mentionner 67
merge — **joindre 109**, rejoindre (se) 109 (118)
mess up — déranger 116
mind — garder 31
mislay — égarer 8
mislead — tromper 31
misrepresent — déformer 31
miss — manquer 103, rater 31
mistaken (be) — méprendre (se) 157 (118), tromper (se) 31 (118)
mistreat — malmener 119
mix — mélanger 116, mêler 31
mix up — confondre 174
moan — gémir 92, râler 31
modernize — moderniser 31
modify — modifier 47
moisten — humecter 100
monitor — contrôler 31
monopolize — monopoliser 31
mop up — éponger 111
motivate — motiver 31
mould — façonner 67, mouler 31
mount — **monter 122**
mourn — pleurer 31
move — bouger 111, déménager 111, déplacer 147, **émouvoir 74**
move apart — écarter 8
move aside — écarter 8

move away éloigner 97
move back reculer 31
move forward **avancer 23**
move in emménager 111
move off démarrer 31, partir 137
move up remonter 122
multiply multiplier 47
mumble marmonner 67
murder assassiner 8, **tuer 202**
murmur murmurer 31

nail clouer 110
name nommer 31
narrate narrer 31
neglect délaisser 154, négliger 111
negociate négocier 15, traiter 31
nibble grignoter 31
nip pincer 147
nod hocher 101
note constater 31, noter 31
note down noter 31
notice remarquer 103
nourish nourrir 92
numb engourdir 92
number numéroter 31

obey **obéir 131**
oblige obliger 111
obscure obscurcir 92
observe observer 8, remarquer 103
obsess obséder 152
obstruct empêcher 8, obstruer 202
obtain **obtenir 132**
occupy occuper 8
occur arriver 19, **passer (se) 139 (118)**
offend offenser 8
offer **offrir 133**, proposer 31
omit omettre 121
open ouvrir 134
operate actionner 67, opérer 156
oppress opprimer 8
opt opter 8
order commander 31
organize organiser 8
orientate orienter 8
oscillate osciller 28
outdo surpasser 154
outline dessiner 31, esquisser 154
outlive survivre 208
outrage indigner 97, scandaliser 31
overcome surmonter 57, **vaincre 203**
overflow déborder 31
overheat surchauffer 8
overload surcharger 111
overpower maîtriser 31
overtake dépasser 154, doubler 31
overthrow renverser 31
overwhelm accabler 8
overwork surmener 119
owe **devoir 62**
own **posséder 152**
own up to avouer 110

pace arpenter 8
pack bourrer 31, remplir 92
pad bourrer 31
pad out étoffer 8
paint **peindre 141**
pamper choyer 129, dorloter 31
panic paniquer 103
pant haleter 3 (101), souffler 31
paralyse paralyser 31
pardon pardonner 67
park garer 31, stationner 67
participate participer 31
pass **passer 139**, réussir 92
pass on communiquer 103, transmettre 121
pat taper 31
pave paver 31
pay **payer 140**, **régler 168**
pay back rembourser 31, **rendre 171**
pay for **payer 140**
pay off amortir 92, désintéresser 154
peak culminer 31
peel éplucher 8, **peler 142**
penetrate **pénétrer 143**
perch percher 31
perfect parfaire 90, perfectionner 67
perforate perforer 31
perform interpréter 35
perish périr 92
permit autoriser 8, **permettre 145**
perpetrate perpétrer 143
persecute persécuter 31

respect respecter 31
respond **répondre 174**
rest reposer 31
restore restaurer 31, restituer 202
restrain retenir 198
restrict restreindre 141
result résulter 31
result in aboutir 92
resume reprendre 157
retain conserver 31, retenir 198
retrain recycler 31
retreat reculer 31
retrieve récupérer 156
return **rendre 171**, **rentrer 172**, **retourner 177**
reveal **découvrir 53**, **révéler 178**
reverse renverser 31, **retourner 177**
review réviser 31
revise réviser 31, **revoir 209**
revive ranimer 31, renaître 170
reward récompenser 31
ride **monter 122**
ridicule ridiculiser 31
ring **appeler 14**, encercler 8, sonner 67
rinse rincer 147
rip déchirer 31
ripen mûrir 92
rise **monter 122**
risk risquer 103
roast rôtir 92
rob dévaliser 31, voler 31
rock bercer 147, osciller 28
roll rouler 31
roll up enrouler 8
rot pourrir 92
rotate tourner 31
rouse soulever 73
row ramer 31
rub frictionner 67, frotter 31
rub out effacer 147
ruin abîmer 8, **détruire 60**, ruiner 31
rule gouverner 31, **régner 169**
rule out éliminer 8, exclure 37
run couler 31, **courir 43**, diriger 111
run away **enfuir (s') 77**, **fuir 96**
run over écraser 8
rush précipiter (se) 31 (118)
rustle frémir 92
sack renvoyer 83
sail naviguer 128, voguer 128
salute saluer 202
salvage récupérer 156, sauver 31
satisfy satisfaire 90
save économiser 8, épargner 97
saw scier 47
say **dire 63**
scald brûler 31
scale escalader 8
scan examiner 8
scare effrayer 140
scatter éparpiller 28, parsemer 185
scent parfumer 31
schedule programmer 31
scold gronder 31
score marquer 103
scorn dédaigner 97
scowl renfrogner (se) 118
scrape racler 31
scratch gratter 31, griffer 31
scream **crier 47**, **hurler 101**
screw visser 154
scribble gribouiller 93, griffonner 67
scrub brosser 154, frotter 31
seal fermer 31, sceller 106
seal off boucler 31, verrouiller 93
search **fouiller 93**
search for chercher 31, rechercher 31
season assaisonner 67
seat **placer 147**
secure assurer 8, garantir 92
seduce séduire 200
see **voir 209**
seek rechercher 31
seem **paraître 136**, sembler 31
seize emparer (s') 118
select sélectionner 67
sell **vendre 205**
send **envoyer 83**
sense pressentir 186, **sentir 186**
separate séparer 31
serve **servir 189**
set fixer 31, **mettre 121**, poser 31
set off **partir 137**
set up établir 92
settle fixer 31, installer (s') 8 (118), **régler 168**

sew **coudre 42**
shake agiter 7, secouer 110, trembler 31
shape façonner 67, modeler 142
share partager 111, répartir 92
sharpen aiguiser 8, tailler 201
shatter éclater 8
shave raser 31
shelter abriter 8
shift bouger 111, déplacer 147
shine **briller 28**, luire 130
shiver frissonner 67
shock choquer 103
shoot tirer 31
shorten raccourcir 92, réduire 200
shout **crier 47**
show montrer 31
shrink rétrécir 92
shut fermer 31
sigh soupirer 31
signpost signaler 31
silence taire 197
simmer mijoter 31
simplify simplifier 47
simulate simuler 31
sin pécher 31
sing **chanter 31**
sink couler 31, sombrer 31
sit **asseoir (s') 21**
situate situer 202
sketch croquer 103, esquisser 154
skid déraper 31
skim **écrémer 71**, effleurer 8
skip sauter 31
skirt border 31
slacken détendre 205
slam claquer 103
slap gifler 31
slaughter abattre 25
sleep **dormir 68**
slide glisser 154
slip glisser 154
slit trancher 31
slow down ralentir 92
slump dégringoler 31
smash fracasser 154
smear barbouiller 93
smell flairer 31, **sentir 186**
smile sourire 180
smoke fumer 31
smooth unir 92
smoulder couver 31
snap craquer 103
sneeze éternuer 202
sniff renifler 31
snore ronfler 31
snow neiger 111
soak tremper 31
soap savonner 67
sob sangloter 31
soften adoucir 92, amollir 92
solve **résoudre 175**
soothe acalmer 31, soulager 111
sort classer 154, trier 47
sow **semer 185**
space out échelonner 67, espacer 147
spare épargner 97
speak parler 31
specialize spécialiser 31
specify préciser 31, spécifier 47
speed up accélérer 156, précipiter 31
spell épeler 14, orthographier 86
spend dépenser 31, **passer 139**
spill renverser 31
spin tourner 31, tournoyer 129
spit cracher 31
splash éclabousser 154
split up partager 111, séparer 31
splutter bredouiller 93
spoil abîmer 8, gâcher 31, gâter 31
sponge éponger 111
spray arroser 8, vaporiser 31
spread étaler 8, **répandre 173**, répartir 92
sprinkle arroser 8
spy on espionner 67
squabble disputer (se) 31 (118), quereller (se) 106 (118)
squash écraser 8
squat (down) accroupir (s') 87
squeeze presser 154
stack empiler 8
stagger chanceler 14
stain tacher 31
stammer bégayer 140
stamp on écraser 8
stand **mettre 121**, supporter 31
stand out ressortir 191 (N)
standardize standardiser 31

unpick découdre 42
unplug débrancher 31
unroll dérouler 31
unscrew dévisser 154
untie dénouer 110
unwind dérouler 31
uphold soutenir 198
upset bouleverser 31, renverser 31
urge encourager 111, presser 154
use employer 129, user 8, utiliser 8

vacate libérer 156, quitter 31
vaccinate vacciner 31
value estimer 8, évaluer 202
vanish disparaître 136
vary diversifier 47, varier 47
venture aventurer (s') 118, hasarder 101
vibrate vibrer 31
view visiter 31
violate violer 31
visit visiter 31
vomit vomir 92
vote voter 31
vow vouer 110

waddle dandiner (se) 118
wail **hurler 101**
wait **attendre 22**, patienter 31
wake (up) réveiller (se) 41 (118)
walk marcher 31
wander errer 188
want **vouloir 210**
ward off obvier 86
warm (up) chauffer 31, tiédir 92
warn avertir 92
wash laver 31
waste gâcher 31, gaspiller 28
watch observer 8, regarder 31
watch out **méfier (se) 118**
water arroser 8
wave agiter 7, brandir 92
waver osciller 28
weaken **affaiblir 6**, faiblir 6
wear porter 31
wear down miner 31, user (s') 8 (118)
wear out épuiser 8, user (s') 8 (118)
weep pleurer 31
weigh **peser 146**
welcome accueillir 2, **recevoir 166**
wet mouiller 93
whine geindre 141
whip fouetter 31
whisk fouetter 31
whisper chuchoter 31
whistle siffler 31
widen élargir 7
win **gagner 97**
wind enrouler 8
wink cligner 97
wipe essuyer 78
wish souhaiter 31
withdraw retirer (se) 31 (118)
wither faner (se) 118, flétrir (se) 92 (118)
withhold retenir 198
withstand résister 31, supporter 31
wobble chanceler 14
work marcher 31, **travailler 201**
work out calculer 31
worry inquiéter (s') 35 (118)
worsen empirer 8
worth (be) **valoir 204**
wound blesser 154
wrap emballer 8
wreck démolir 92, **détruire 60**
wrestle lutter 31
wring tordre 123
wring out essorer 8
wrinkle froncer 11
write **écrire 72**
wrong **léser 114**

yawn bâiller 201
yell **hurler 101**

zigzag zigzaguer 128